The best football player you never heard of, who dashed across the gridiron for just one season, long ago.
—**Frank Deford,** *Sports Illustrated* and Hall of Fame sportswriter; NPR *Morning Edition* commentator; author of *Everybody's All-American,* *Bliss Remembered,* and *Alex: The Life of a Child*

Here's a great storyteller, Bill Chastain, with an oversized story to tell, about a mighty mite of a legend back when legends mattered, a high school and college sensation whose candle burned so bright – and quickly. And about a time, a time just like now, when young hearts, with all those dreams inside, went to fight a war and never came back. Clint Castleberry died 66 years ago. He lives in these pages.
—Martin Fennelly, ***The Tampa Tribune***

Clint Castleberry's story is one that impacted Georgia Tech and college football in the south. Bill Chastain does a great job of capturing this unique American hero.
—Wes Durham, **Director of Broadcasting, "Voice of the Yellow Jackets"**

Also by Bill Chastain

Nonfiction

September Nights: Hunting the Beasts of the American League East

Hack's 191: Hack Wilson's Incredible 1930 Season

The Steve Spurrier Story: From Heisman to Head Ball Coach

Payne at Pinehurst: The Greatest U.S. Open Ever

Steel Dynasty: The Team that Changed the NFL

Purpose and Passion: Bobby Pruett and the Marshall Years

100 Things Jets Fans Should Know and Do Before They Die

100 Things Giants Fans Should Know and Do Before They Die

Fiction

The Streak

Peachtree Corvette Club

JACKRABBIT

Clint Castleberry wearing a practice jersey instead of his #19 game jersey.

JACKRABBIT

The Story of
Clint Castleberry
and the Improbable
1942 Georgia Tech Football Season

Bill Chastain

Foreword by Tony Barnhart

cadent PUBLISHING

Printed in the United States of America

Copyright © 2011 by Bill Chastain

Library of Congress Control Number: 2011943455

ISBN 9781937644055 (pbk)
ISBN 9781937644062 (eBook)

Cover and interior design by Janet Robbins, North Wind Design & Production, www.nwdpbooks.com

Cover, frontispiece, page 20, page 197 photo credit: Copyright Georgia Institute of Technology. Photo on page 205 by Pam Dickens. All other text photos courtesy Special Collections and Archives, Georgia State University Library,

Cadent Publishing
9 Gleason Street
Thomaston, ME 04861

www.cadentpublishing.com

To Pops.

I'll never quit missing you. I love you and think about you every day.

Contents

Foreword by Tony Barnhart 11
Prologue 13

1   Football at Georgia Tech 17
2   Bobby Dodd and Years of Losing 35
3   Boys' High and Shorty Doyal 47
4   A Local Talent 53
5   Boys' High Finale 65
6   America at War 73
7   Will there be a Season? 85
8   A Freshman Opens Eyes 91
9   A Monster in Athens 99
10   A Freshmen Sensation Arrives 105
11   On to South Bend 110
12   Undefeated and Coach Aleck in Poor Health 118
13   Anchors Away 124
14   Duke and the Rest of the Field 130
15   Dodd Takes Over 134
16   Crimson Tide Crossroads 140
17   One More Before Georgia 150
18   The Much-Awaited Showdown 155
19   Honors and the Cotton Bowl 172
20   Winter of the Crazed Jackrabbit 180

Epilogue 189
Acknowledgments 199
Sources 201
Author 205

Foreword

I learned a long time ago that some of the best and most interesting stories in college football are not about what *was,* but rather what might have been if history or circumstances had taken a different turn.

College football is full of stories about individuals who were simply in the right place at the right time with the right amount of talent to achieve success. There are countless others who appeared destined for stardom but, because of bad fortune or fate, never had a chance to fulfill their dreams.

And there is a third group, a very small group. These are men who had their journey to glory cut short but achieved immortality anyway. That's because, in the short time they were here, their stars burned white-hot, and nothing—not even death—could extinguish their flames.

Clint Castleberry was such a man, and in this book Bill Chastain expertly crafts one of the great "what-if" stories in college football history.

Castleberry was already a football legend before he got to Georgia Tech in 1942. Chastain takes the reader back to one of the great periods of high school football, when the rivalry between Atlanta's Boys' High and Tech High was all the rage. It was a simpler, more innocent time, and Chastain captures it perfectly.

Bill not only tells us the story of an All-America player and an all-American boy, he gives us a new look at some of the legendary names in Georgia Tech history and how they came to have an impact on the Castleberry story.

If you know Georgia Tech or college football, you certainly know the names of John Heisman, William Alexander, and Bobby Dodd. In this book Chastain gives new details on what made these men tick and how they built one of the greatest traditions in college football history.

In just one unforgettable college football season, the autumn of 1942, Clint Castleberry positioned himself to become one of the greatest players of all time. National championships were possible. At least one Heisman Trophy was all but certain. But as much as Castleberry loved college football, he loved his country more and was honor-bound to leave college and go defend it. In 1944 his plane disappeared off the African coast and was never found. His loss left a gap in Georgia Tech's football legacy that remains unfilled even today.

The story of Clint Castleberry is really the story of our Greatest Generation, and Bill Chastain tells it with loving detail. You will be entertained. If you remember those days, you'll shed a tear or two. And if you love college football history, I promise you will learn a lot. I know I did.

Enjoy.

Tony Barnhart

Prologue

Patriotism fueled a country at war in 1942. Pearl Harbor had changed everything. America had little appetite for war before December 7, 1941, but after that day, fright and vulnerability stoked the country's fervor to meet the enemy. If the Japanese could attack Pearl Harbor, further attacks might take place on the mainland, and Germany's war machine—directed by a madman—looked even more imposing than the Empire of the Rising Sun. The consequences of defeat didn't bear thinking about.

Convinced that victory was essential to preserve America and the American way of life, the nation's citizens were inspired to do whatever seemed necessary to help the war effort. Scrap drives collected millions of tons of metal, rubber, and newspapers. Businesses redirected resources to the production of war materiel and support of the war effort. General Motors ceased car production and dedicated 100 percent of its production to the manufacture of military engines, trucks, tanks, airplanes, and more, with a total price tag of more than $12 billion. Sacrifice and denial moved forefront in the national psyche. Getting more out of less became the ruling mantra.

Prior to the 1942 season, college football appeared likely to become one more cherished pastime the country could do without while attending to the grim business of war, not least because so many college gridiron players and coaches had enlisted in the armed forces and were in basic training or already overseas. Those left behind wondered if the season should be played. Would there be enough players remaining to fill a competitive roster? Would the games be worth watching? Would playing games while young men in uniform fought and died be unpatriotic?

But a country that could play football at home while fighting two powerful enemies overseas must be a strong country indeed. Let the Germans and Japanese take note, and let our own boys in uniform take solace from the sports news back home. Such considerations weighed heavily in favor of a college football season.

Keeping the sport alive despite the many departed athletes and coaches presented a monumental challenge, and it prompted a ruling that allowed college freshmen to participate in varsity sports for only the second time, the first having been during World War I. The season was on, but it was on trial as well. If the sport—more nearly a religion in the South—was to survive during World War II, the 1942 season had to prove worthy of the effort.

The ruling enabled one freshman in particular, Clinton Dillon Castleberry, Jr., to burst onto the college football scene after enrolling at Georgia Tech.

Standing five-foot-nine and weighing 155 pounds, Castleberry was a young man of merely ordinary size in a game dominated by giants, but he had speed to burn, lightning quickness, instinctive talent, and immense heart. Upon entering Tech he had never lost a football game—and he had played many against tough opponents. The string continued in the fall of 1942.

A shotgun wedding between the ball carrier who ran like a "crazed jackrabbit" and the still-growing magic of radio created an unlikely hero who captured the hearts and imaginations of Atlanta, the Eastern seaboard, and, by the end of the 1942 season, an entire country. Castleberry's exploits became a national obsession at home and abroad. He was the real-life Chip Hilton six years before Clair Bee's first chronicle of the fictional sports hero was published in 1948. The Armed Forces Radio Service carried "Fibber McGee and Molly," President Roosevelt's fireside chats, and weekly broadcasts featuring the decided underdog from Georgia who each Saturday performed his David act on the next Goliath standing in his way.

Castleberry disappeared from football after the 1942 season. Like a lot of other young men who went off to fight in World War II and made the ultimate sacrifice, he left behind a young widow, a grief-struck family, and desolate friends all asking themselves the saddest question: What if? Castleberry left something for Georgia Tech fans, too—hazy memories of halcyon fall afternoons and effervescent glory.

Castleberry's name has retained a mythical quality on the Georgia Tech campus and in the city of Atlanta. Many have heard of him, but few know his story.

The story begins with the legendary John Heisman, who coached football at Georgia Tech from 1903 through 1919, four years before Castleberry was born. It leads next to a precocious dreamer, William Alexander, who wanted to be a doctor but ended up becoming Heisman's successor at Georgia Tech and one of the greatest coaches in college football history. Coach Aleck directed the Tech team until 1945 before passing it along to his understudy, Bobby Dodd, who ushered in a golden era of Yellow Jacket football over the next two decades. Both Alexander and Dodd coached Castleberry in his brief, blazing arc across the college gridiron.

Nor would the story of Georgia Tech football and Castleberry's place in it be complete if it failed to note the grand football legacy of Tech's host city, Atlanta. For two decades, beginning in 1925, that legacy flowed through Boys' High in Atlanta, where R.L. "Shorty" Doyal, himself a legend, coached Castleberry and other legends of the game.

We begin at the beginning.

1

Football at Georgia Tech

College admissions had a distinctly subjective flavor in the early 1900s. Scholastic aptitude tests had not yet been developed, which left the fate of a prospective student's application to the halls of higher learning in the hands of an administrator. For William Anderson Alexander, that turned out to be a good thing. When he walked into the Georgia Tech registrar's office in 1906 and declared his intention to study engineering, the 16-year-old from Mud River, Kentucky, lacked the required high school education to be admitted to the esteemed engineering school in downtown Atlanta, but what he lacked in academic background he more than made up in persistence. By the time Alexander left the registrar's office, he had been admitted to Tech as an apprentice student.

Alexander's parents, Luther and Gertrude, had met in Gertrude's hometown of Nashville, where Luther, the son of a Presbyterian minister, taught a Sunday school class. Gertrude Anderson had graduated from college—Peabody Normal—and combined a keen mind with an irresistible beauty. Luther Alexander was smitten from their first meeting, and soon they began to plan a life together. Sharing a desire to serve others, they mapped out a future in which they would travel to China to become missionaries. After marrying, however, the couple put their plans on hold at the request of Gertrude's father, William Green Smith Anderson, who asked for Luther's help managing a coal mine in which he was heavily invested. Convinced that Luther could help Anderson in his time of need, Luther and Gertrude accompanied her parents to Mud River. Before they knew it, one year had turned into six, and their dreams of becoming missionaries had faded away.

That unfulfilled dream did not affect the erudite couple's happiness, though. They lived with the Andersons in a large wood-frame double-occupancy house that Gertrude's father had built. Life was good for the couple, and soon they had a son, William, and a daughter, Elizabeth.

A beautiful child with long, dark eyelashes, William by age five proved irresistible to female neighbors and guests, who showered him with hugs and affection. He grew to loathe the attention and began to shy away from contact with the opposite sex, a precursor to his adult diffidence toward women. He would retreat to the woods when female relatives or friends were scheduled to come by the house. On one occasion William coaxed Elizabeth into accompanying him with a blanket and food, determined to spend the night in the woods if need be to avoid the torments of unwanted affection at home. Luther eventually noticed that his children were missing and went into the woods on horseback to find them. Only when the stubborn William received a promise that he would not be kissed did he relent and return home with his father.

William displayed a sense of honor as early as age six when, after misbehaving, he was told by his father—who was home only briefly during lunch break from the mine—that he would be punished at the end of the day. By the time Luther returned home in the evening, he had forgotten all about William's misbehavior, but William had not. Dutifully he reported to his father with hair combed and face washed.

"Here I am, Papa," William said. "You said you were going to whip me at six o'clock."

Luther, who adhered to stern Presbyterian principles, followed through, spanking his son.

Halcyon days for the Alexander family were interrupted by a string of disasters. First a fire destroyed their home, burning virtually every possession the couple owned including furniture, books, clothing, and even the family silverware. Losing the house prompted a succession of moves from one farmhouse to another before the family moved into a company-owned house.

Misfortunes began to riddle the mine as well—the family's only source of income. The tipple, or surface structures, burned twice and had to be rebuilt. Later the mine flooded, and the cost of continually pumping out the water rivaled the price they were getting for the coal, eventually forcing them to abandon the mine. Just prior to the mine's closing, the Alexander family received the most devastating news of all: Luther had contracted tuberculosis.

In the absence of sanitariums in the late 1800s, Luther continued to work until he could no longer walk. Hoping to address his declining health with proper medical care, the couple moved to Luther's parents' home in Nashville, which is where he died in 1895.

A mother of two facing life as a widow, Gertrude knew she had to find a way to make a living. Teaching was her answer. She taught throughout the state of Georgia at Peabody in Macon; Cox College, a private women's college in College Park; and finally in the State Normal School at Athens.

Once the school year concluded, Gertrude would gather her children and head back to Mud River to spend time with her parents. Like most rural communities in the late 1890s, Mud River had no electricity. (Even forty years later only 10% of rural American homes were electrified, a hardship addressed by President Franklin Roosevelt through the Rural Electrification Administration beginning in 1935.) The atmosphere in the small town gave William and Elizabeth a healthy alternative to city life while helping to shape their young and evolving minds. William enjoyed fishing and hunting and felt at home in the outdoors.

The siblings loved the mountain children of Mud River, naïve in many respects but independent, quick-witted, and possessed of personalities that made William and Elizabeth's city friends seem bland in contrast. This varied upbringing gave balance to William's life and taught him something about the sources and nature of good character. William learned to identify pretentiousness as one of the more distasteful traits of human nature. Having been around those who had little, he gained an understanding and empathy for the underprivileged.

William Alexander fought his way into Tech as a student, managed to earn a spot on the football team, and later became the school's second head football coach.

William Alexander displayed a zeal for learning and dreamed of becoming a doctor. Upon finding a dated medical book entitled *Family Physician* at his grandfather's home one summer, he devoured the contents, allowing his photographic memory to absorb all things big and small in the realm of medicine. At age 12 he put his knowledge to work, administering a homemade splint to a family cat that had broken its leg. Miraculously, the cat recovered. But the dream of becoming a doctor eventually gave way to the somewhat more attainable one of becoming an engineer, a decision he did not reach without careful deliberation. William knew that becoming a doctor would require four years of college followed by four years of medical school and two years of being an intern or working at a clinic. His mother dearly wished for him to go to college, yet he wanted to begin earning a living as soon as possible. Thus he decided he'd be best served by pursuing an engineering degree at Georgia Tech.

Alexander entered college as a decided underdog. Gertrude's teaching profession had occasioned frequent relocations throughout his childhood. Ironically, the itinerant teacher's devotion to her profession proved detrimental to her own children's education. Fortunately for Alexander, Tech had established the Apprentice Class to serve the many applicants who had attained less than adequate high school educations.

Grudgingly, he paid for school with money given to him by his mother. He knew she needed the money, but she insisted it would be better put to use paying for his education. Throughout college he carried a pocket notebook in which he kept a neat accounting of his finances. Between the covers of that notebook, Alexander wrote down every penny he received from her so he could repay her once he began to earn a living.

Tech's stringent guidelines for its students were set forth in the school's student handbook. Rooms were to be in order, beds made up, floors swept, and students dressed at 6:40 A.M., when the inspection bell rang. Any student found with intoxicating liquors in his possession would be suspended from school. Students were required to patronize the laundry. Absences of all students were mailed to parents weekly. Any student found engaging in disorderly or boisterous conduct, or whistling, or running through the halls or shops, or smoking in any building except the dormitories would receive such penalties as the faculty might direct. Each student was to have two suits of overalls costing about $1 each. Athletic teams were not allowed to visit other places except to play games with educational institutions.

Such discipline and restrictions were accepted in that era and did nothing to deter Alexander's love of the Atlanta school.

The attractive child had become a handsome young man. He possessed a shock of curly chestnut hair, and dimples appeared on his cheeks when he smiled. He might have been a ladies' man except that he retained the shyness of his youth around women. As a boy he had escaped ladies by disappearing into the woods; now he disappeared into thin air whenever his fraternity, Kappa Sigma, held a dance.

Predictably, Alexander struggled in the classroom. He spent two years in the freshman class alone. According to records from Tech's

John Heisman put Georgia Tech football on the map as the school's first head football coach before leaving his post after getting a divorce. Years later the trophy bearing his name would honor college football's best player.

Office of the Registrar, he made a 42 in Math 25—calculus—before retaking the course and rebounding with a 77. In Math 26, he first earned a 31 before hiking that to a 69 the next time out. And he received an initial 41 in Physics 20 before raising that to an 87 on his second attempt.

By the time Alexander turned 18 he had progressed enough in the classroom to be enrolled as a regular Georgia Tech student. His struggles in the classroom carried over to the football team, where, in essence, he served as a tackling dummy. He lacked size, speed, and talent. What he did have were persistence and heart. Alexander never missed a practice during the 1906 and 1907 seasons, which is miraculous given his slender build and the passion he brought to practice.

Tech's football coach, John Heisman, called his squad together at the outset of the 1908 season and began to offer the ins and outs of how he saw the season unfolding and how the team would reach the goals he had set for them. Then he announced the eleven players who would comprise his first string, playing both offense and defense while wearing leather helmets with less padding than a catcher's mitt. Heisman's memorable meeting eventually reached a juncture that is familiar to this day to every kid who has never been picked to play in a neighborhood football game. The Tech coach singled out the half-dozen or so players who would compete with the first string to try and unseat them. After those selections were made, only a few freshmen and the "scrubs" such as Alexander remained unselected. At that point, Heisman perused the faces of the remaining players and spoke.

"There's old Aleck. What shall we do with him?"

Heisman had not intended for anybody to answer, but Chip Robert, the team captain, weighed in.

"Coach, why not make old Aleck captain of the scrubs? He's never absent. He's always in the way of the varsity ball carrier. He's always at the bottom of the pile-up."

Heisman considered Robert's suggestion and pronounced, "Aleck, you are now captain of the scrub team. You are in charge. I will deal with it through you."

College eligibility restrictions were not far advanced at this stage, and Alexander remained captain of the scrub team through the 1911 season. Staying on as he did allowed him to show an ability that served Heisman better than anything Alexander could have done on the field: he began to scout Tech's opponents. Scouting allowed Alexander to incorporate his mind into an evolving game. He displayed a knack for deciphering what other teams were doing, why they were successful, and what would be the best way to stop them or score points against them. Alexander turned what he learned into detailed reports that Heisman could use while preparing to face those opponents.

Alexander never starred on the gridiron—far from it—yet he found success of a different sort through persistence and hard work. Despite having poor hands and two left feet, Alexander earned Heisman's respect, so much so that the crusty coach overlooked the young man's shortcomings and allowed him to see action in the Georgia and Clemson games during his senior season. Alexander played enough downs to become a letterman—a happy outcome likely motivated by the plans Heisman was harboring for Alexander after his playing days were complete.

Six years after setting foot in the registrar's office at Georgia Tech, Alexander graduated with a B.S. degree in civil engineering in 1912. Amazingly, he graduated as class valedictorian, though school records show that he was nowhere near the top of his class. Researchers at the Georgia Tech Department of Living History believe that he must have been selected for the honor based on his popularity. That no valedictorians were designated in earlier or later classes suggests that Alexander's fellow students had a special reason for bestowing the title on him.

Shortly after graduation, Alexander accepted a position as a mathematics instructor at Georgia Tech. In addition to his teaching duties, he filled a slot as an assistant coach for the legendary Heisman.

     • • • • •

The Heisman family name had an inauspicious beginning in America.

Johann Michael von Bogart hailed from Germany, the son of Baron von Bogart, of German nobility. When Johann fell in love with a girl of limited means from Alsace-Lorraine, his father would have nothing more to do with his son. So once the couple married, Johann assumed his wife's name, Heisman, and moved to America.

Their son and future legendary coach John Wilhelm Heisman was born in Cleveland in 1869 and first embraced football at Brown University before transferring to the University of Pennsylvania to earn a law degree. While at Penn, a tragic incident turned into a boon for college football when Heisman's eyes were damaged from Madison Square Garden's galvanic lighting system while he was playing in an indoor game for Penn. Doctors prescribed rest for his eyes, so he navigated away from the law books and started listening to his heart instead. His heart told him he should coach football.

His first college coaching opportunity came at Oberlin College in Ohio. Stints followed at Buchtel College (now the University of Akron), Oberlin again, then Alabama Polytechnic Institute (now Auburn). Heisman's crafty innovations to the evolving game of football attracted notice from those who played, coached, and followed the game. He first used the hidden ball trick when Alabama Polytechnic Institute played Vanderbilt. The condensed version saw

Heisman's quarterback stuff the ball under his jersey, then bend down as if to tie his shoe. Once the defense had been misdirected elsewhere, the quarterback scored without being touched.

Heisman moved on to coach at Clemson, where he also pursued his interest in acting and became involved in local theater productions, several of which were Shakespearean dramas. Examining the dark expression on Heisman's face in old photographs, one can easily envision him reciting "to be, or not to be" with grave seriousness during a production of Hamlet. Heisman met his first wife, Evelyn McCollum Cox, while acting, and she occasionally acted in the same plays with him. Much to Heisman's chagrin, his mastery of the English language and his oratorical skills served him less well on the stage than the football field; his range as an actor was said to be limited.

Georgia Tech brought Heisman aboard on Thanksgiving Day 1903, setting off a celebration by happy Tech students who unfurled a banner proclaiming, "Tech Gets Heisman for 1904." Tech hired their first-ever paid coach for an annual salary of $2,250 and 30 percent of the net gate receipts. Understanding where his bread would be buttered, Heisman immediately got to work developing a football team worth the price of admission.

Convict labor provided by the city of Atlanta cleared a parcel of flat land on the campus just east of the Georgia Tech administration building, then constructed a fence around it. It wasn't fancy, but it was a place for the team to play and fans to buy tickets. By 1905, the Tech team played its home games on this area known as "The Flats." This primitive venue ushered in a glorious era of Tech football, with their innovative coach leading the way. Later, in 1913, the concrete stadium known as Grant Field was erected by student labor.

Heisman remained on the cutting edge of an evolving game with innovations such as refining the use of lateral and backward passes, reverses, onside kicks, and using a pulling guard on sweeps. Infatuated with the forward pass, he became a vocal proponent of legalizing this innovation to change the face of the game and reduce its level of violence.

In 1905, college football experienced eighteen deaths and 151 serious injuries. During a press conference at the White House on October 5, 1905, President Theodore Roosevelt called for the game to be reformed but not abolished. The president's interest led to a rules committee being formed on January 12, 1906, and the committee legalized the forward pass, established a neutral zone between the offensive and defensive lines, and adopted a rule that required a team to gain 10 yards in four downs in order to keep possession of the football. Heisman embraced the changes, and his keen football mind quickly allowed him to employ them to his advantage.

A strict disciplinarian, Heisman did not tolerate profanity or misbehavior. Execution bloomed from this adherence to discipline, which led his teams to a dependence on speed and precise maneuvers. The "Heisman shift," which he first used at Tech, has been recognized as the precursor to the "T" and "I" formations. And his teams did not huddle—rather, they lined up immediately after a play as in a modern no-huddle offense. Under Heisman, who came to be called "The Wizard," Tech grew into a national football power, building a gridiron legacy. One game against Cumberland University in 1916 might be passed off as urban legend were its outcome not well-reported and easily verified.

Located in Lebanon, Tennessee, Cumberland had used professional baseball players from a Nashville team to stomp Tech's baseball team 22 – 0 in the spring of 1916. So angered by this were Tech alumni and students that an outcry arose for an opportunity to avenge the embarrassment. No doubt with his share of gate receipts in mind, Heisman took it upon himself to provide such an opportunity by offering a $500 guarantee to Cumberland if they would bring a football team to Atlanta to play the Yellow Jackets in the fall.

Cumberland had been a football powerhouse in 1903 and 1904, but the school's main focus had since become its law school, and its gridiron fortunes had subsided dramatically. By 1916 just sixteen young men played for the team. That group understood they were in for a whipping in Atlanta, so they sought reinforcements along the way. As the Bulldogs traveled south by train, they stopped in Nashville and tried to recruit players from Vanderbilt's football team. Their effort failed, and instead they lost three players, who opted not to continue to Atlanta. The game had all the trappings of a Tech rout, but nobody could have predicted what happened.

Tech scored 63 points in the first quarter, prompting Cumberland's decision to kick the football back to Tech right after receiving the next kickoff. By halftime Tech led 126 – 0, and a decision was made to reduce the remaining quarters from 15 to 12 minutes. The final score was Tech 222, Cumberland 0.

Late in the game a Cumberland player left the field and took a seat on the Tech bench. A perplexed Heisman confronted the player and told him he was on the wrong bench, but the player promptly replied that he was on the right bench. Heisman walked away bemused, then returned and once again told the player he was not on the right bench. Still the player made no motion to leave, and finally Heisman addressed the youngster in a stern manner.

"Son, you are on the wrong bench!" Heisman said.

"I'm on the right bench," the player shot back. "If I go back over there, they'll put me in again. I've been in five times already and that's enough."

Heisman's Tech teams continued to enjoy great success, going undefeated in 1917 en route to the school's first national championship. During this period Tech experienced a 33-game undefeated streak in which they outscored their opponents 1,599 to 99. Not as well remembered as the rout of Cumberland were some of the other one-sided scores compiled by Tech during that streak. In 1917, Tech defeated Vanderbilt 83 – 0 and Carlisle 98 – 0, and in 1918 they beat Furman 118 – 0, the 11th Calvary 123 – 0, and North Carolina State 128 – 0.

* * * * *

William Alexander remained in his dual role as mathematics instructor and football coach for five years after accepting the job in 1912, bringing an indisputable value to Heisman's teams. The pair's strengths appeared to be a perfect match. A creative genius, Heisman brought concepts to the table, while the detail-oriented Alexander meticulously tied up Heisman's loose ends. Alexander is also believed to have opened Heisman's eyes to the value of a solid defense.

During scouting trips in which he had watched Auburn, Alexander took note of how their coach, Mike Donahue, focused primarily on stopping the other team. Alexander had an appreciation for defense based on his years as a scrub, during which he had used various closing angles and coverage and tackling techniques while trying to stop athletes of far greater ability. In contrast, Heisman favored the offensive side of the ball and felt that an aggressive, constantly attacking offense was what drove the train. While Heisman incorporated many of Alexander's beliefs into his football team, he remained the marquee attraction. Alexander and his contributions remained in the background, which never seemed to bother the introverted Alexander.

Alexander left Tech in June 1918 to enlist in the ambulance corps during World War I. Disappointed that he did not get sent overseas, he transferred to the field artillery, which proved to be his ticket to France. After taking a ninety-day course on how to handle a 155-millimeter gun, he passed tests in operating procedures and target firing before reluctantly becoming a teacher. He requested a transfer to the field as the American offensive gathered itself, but his commander turned down the request, telling him he had more value as an instructor. So he earned a commission as a second lieutenant while instructing troops on the finer points of mathematics at a field artillery school near St. Aignan, France.

A life-changing circumstance for Alexander came upon the conclusion of World War I. He received a directive to coach a football team while the slow process of demobilization got underway, and his team earned distinction as one of the best football teams in France. This success, for the first time, gave him clarity about his future. For as far back as he could remember, he had struggled to identify his path in life. Now he recognized that the answer had been right in front of him. Coaching soldiers on a football field in France, he saw his life's work staring back at him. Coaching ran through his blood, and the profession appealed to him as his best avenue for success. Returning to Tech in 1919, Alexander rejoined Heisman's coaching staff.

* * * * *

Following the 1919 season, in which Tech posted a 7 – 3 record, Heisman called together the members of Tech's athletic board to join him at his house for lunch. Once they finished eating, Heisman stood and spoke.

"Gentlemen, you are my closest friends in Atlanta, and I am indebted for your loyalty and confidence," Heisman said. "It is with regret that I inform you Mrs. Heisman and I have agreed to separate. It is a personal matter, there are no hard feelings, and there is understanding. We have taken everything into consideration."

Heisman went on to say that the separation had brought with it the realization that the couple could no longer live in the same city. He concluded by dropping the bomb: Since Mrs. Heisman wanted to remain in Atlanta, Tech needed to look for a new football coach. Heisman had three years left on his contract with Georgia Tech when he resigned to become the coach at the University of Pennsylvania.

Heisman's shocking departure prompted Tech to proclaim its intention to hire a "big name" coach, but Tech's football players had other ideas. They wanted Alexander to be the choice, and the school finally caved after a little blackmail. If Tech chose to continue its search for a big-time coach and did not hire Alexander, the players threatened that the school would also have to field a new football team. Drama aside, Alexander—a devout Heisman disciple—had the perfect resumé to succeed his mentor. He understood every coaching innovation Heisman had ever introduced at Tech and had been on hand when Heisman had implemented it. All Alexander needed was an opportunity. Making him head coach ensured a smooth transition after Heisman's departure.

Any doubts about Alexander's ability to coach were quickly put to rest during his first season, when Tech lost just one game. A memorable two-week period during the 1920 season saw Alexander play his second team the entire game in a 7 – 0 win at Clemson so he could rest the first team for the following week's game against powerhouse Centre College. Tech then defeated Centre 24 – 0, marking the first time the Colonels had been held scoreless in five years.

Alexander didn't fit the stereotypical image of the gum-chewing, whistle-blowing, blood-and-guts football coach. He possessed a great sense of humor, enjoyed reading, and his reserved but stern manner suggested a scholarly sort, which served him well at an engineering school with stringent academic standards. Tech football players found a different scene with Alexander in charge.

Heisman had worked his teams hard during practices. If they weren't scrimmaging, the taskmaster had the team stay in condition by employing a forty-foot hill behind the athletic offices. Two waist-high trenches cut in the hill allowed players to run through the trenches up and down the hill until exhaustion consumed them. Alexander believed in scrimmaging and conditioning, but he tried to save his players for the game.

Said one player from the 1920 team: "It was a drastic change from the coaching of Heisman. Aleck made you like the game of football, and it ceased to be a punishing grind. And instead of fiery orations by the eloquent Heisman, we were treated to low-keyed talks that relaxed our tensions before we went on the field."

Not until Alexander's fifth year on the job did the Yellow Jackets lose to a Southern team, and he did not shy away from tough opponents. He made clear the direction he wanted to take the program by scheduling Tech to play Notre Dame from 1922 to 1929. He explained his logic for instituting such a series by noting: "They will beat us about nine times out of ten, but in losing we will learn a lot of football. We will gain a lot of prestige nationally. And when we win, it will be a mighty sweet victory."

Alexander's words were prophetic. Notre Dame indeed ruled the series, losing to Tech only once in those years, 13 – 0 in 1928. And, as Alexander had predicted, that victory led to national prestige.

Tech finished the 1928 season with a 9 – 0 record, including a 7 – 0 mark in the Southern Conference (the precursor to the Southeastern Conference), to earn a spot in the Rose Bowl against the University of California on New Year's Day of 1929. Of all the special moments during that game—which came to be known as "the granddaddy of them all"—one in particular proved most unusual.

Georgia Tech halfback Stumpy Thomason was hit hard by California's Benny Lom at the Tech 35 early in the second quarter. Thomason couldn't hold onto the ball, and it popped into the air. The Golden Bears' Roy Riegels grabbed the football and took off up the field—only he headed toward the wrong end zone. Lom pursued Riegels, shouting at him to turn around, but the plea did not register with Riegels, who replied, "Get away from me, this is my touchdown."

Alexander remained calm amid the chaos on the field, instructing his team to do the same, telling them: "Every step he takes is to our advantage."

The faster Lom caught Riegels at the California 1, where they were quickly joined by a host of Tech players. Photographs appear to show Riegels getting tackled in the end zone for what would have been a safety, but eventually the officials placed the ball at the 1-yard line. Tech held California, then blocked a punt for a safety en route to an 8 – 7 win, Tech's first-ever in a bowl game. Tech was recognized as national champion by a consensus of the polls available at the time. A crowd of 100,000 greeted the team on Peachtree Street upon its return to Atlanta. Riegels left Pasadena with the moniker he would carry until his death in 1993: "Wrong Way" Roy Riegels.

Alexander gained the respect of his peers. Among them, Knute Rockne—the coach of Notre Dame and one of the greatest coaches in college football history—could be counted as one of his closest coaching friends. It was Rockne who said, "Bill Alexander gets more out of less than any coach in America."

Alexander came to be known around the country as a master football technician. He preferred diagramming plays for his players to fire-and-brimstone speeches or inspirational pep talks. He believed that playing with a player's emotions promoted mental instability.

Time Magazine wrote of Alexander, "No man to keep his opinions to himself, he argued doggedly against the huddle (because it slowed the game), and once brushed off a proposal for fancy new uniforms with a terse: 'You look mighty silly when you lose in a trick getup.'"

Alexander had an endearing way about him, though his behavior could be quirky. During the days when he served as a mathematics instructor at Tech, one of his students sought him out the day before final exams to tell him that he needed to pass the class or he would flunk out. Alexander's advice—which came during Prohibition years—was to procure some whiskey.

"You get yourself an ice cream soda glass, fill it with Georgia corn, and in a few minutes your mind will work like an adding machine," Alexander told his student.

When Alexander administered the exam the following day, the

young man signed his name to the blue test booklet, then tucked it under his arm and left the room. Later that day Alexander saw the boy and asked him what had happened.

"Coach, after following your instructions I didn't give a damn whether I took the exam or not," the boy replied.

At one time Alexander roomed with D.M. Smith, who became a teaching legend at Tech. When asked about that experience, Smith replied: "He only owns one pair of sheets and one pair of pajamas. When the sheets are in the laundry he uses his pajamas, and when his pajamas are in the laundry he sleeps between the sheets. I would like to have a fellow that at least had one more pair of sheets and one more pair of pajamas."

During a game between Tech and Notre Dame at Grant Field, Tech player Bob Randolph had his front tooth knocked out, leaving the nerve of the missing tooth exposed. Alexander needed Randolph to continue playing, but any hint of a breeze to the nerve caused Randolph excruciating pain. Alexander's solution was to pluck out his chewing gum and use it to cap Randolph's exposed nerve. When Randolph told Alexander one stick of gum wasn't going to last him the entire game, Alexander handed out gum to his reserves and had them begin chewing replacement gum for the remainder of the game.

Tech's players loved the way "Coach Aleck" diagrammed a football play—he used small X's for Tech players on the chalkboard and large O's for opposing players—and they loved the way he coddled them after a loss. When they won, he did what was necessary to keep their hat sizes the same, even chastising them to do so. And he always stuck up for his players. In one episode, Coach Aleck walked into the locker room after a loss to find a trainer berating the team. Coach Aleck told the man, "This isn't your team except when it wins. It's just lost a game, and it's my team. Get out . . . before I throw you out."

Coach Aleck presided over Tech like an owl perched above the campus, seeing everything and wisely processing what he saw. Occasionally that diligence paid off with an uncovered treasure like F.O. Waddey, who left Memphis in the fall of 1925 to enroll at Tech as a co-operative student. The co-op program at Tech served its students well, giving them an education as well as work experience while they were in school. Any student enrolled in this program would go to school a semester, then work a semester, which allowed the student to make extra money to pay for his schooling while also acquiring the necessary practical tools to hit the real world running after college.

A bachelor who lived where he worked, Coach Aleck would occasionally take in an intramural football game when he had the time. Rolling around in the back of his mind would be the memory of how joining the football team as a student had served him at Tech, enhancing his college experience and making him a more well-rounded student. Watching intramural football provided him a release in addition to feeding his belief that a future Tech football player could be hidden away on the intramural fields. Waddey proved to be such an animal. Coach Aleck liked several of the traits displayed by the young man. He could run a little bit, but more than anything else he had fearlessness and style. So after watching Waddey on more than one occasion, Coach Aleck spoke to him.

"Come out for spring practice. We have equipment for you."

In a similar fashion, Coach Aleck discovered E.J. Crowley, who became the captain of the 1927 team. Thanks to his diligence, Coach Aleck ended up with a pair of coveted ends in Waddey and Crowley.

After winning the national championship in 1928, Tech followed with just three wins in 1929, yet Coach Aleck's stock remained high in the coaching profession. Wallace Wade resigned his post at Alabama on January 1, 1930, to become the head coach at Duke. By that summer, Alabama still had not found a new head coach, but they knew who they wanted. An Alabama contingent led by school president Dr. George H. Denny offered Coach Aleck the position. Despite knowing that a move to Tuscaloosa would mean excellent players while also doubling his salary, Coach Aleck opted to remain at Tech.

"I am not sure I would be a good coach at Alabama," Coach Aleck said. "In fact, I am pretty sure I would not be. I am not sure I would be a good coach anywhere except here at Georgia Tech. Come to think of it, I'm not sure I am a good coach here, but I am going to stay as long as I can. Some think that won't be long. We lost five games last year and won only three. That's a comedown from the Rose Bowl, and it looks as though it might be as bad this fall."

Coach Aleck surmised with a chuckle: "That would put Dr. Denny in a worse fix than he is in now."

Coach Aleck's words about the 1930 season proved prophetic when Tech won just two games. Nobody liked losing, but a losing season, or even several in a row, did not seal a coach's fate in those days as it would decades later. Coach Aleck remained Tech's coach and kept his sense of humor intact.

John Bascom Crenshaw served as a professor on the Tech faculty and coached Tech's lacrosse team. A passionate promoter of lacrosse, he struggled to find any humor in Coach Aleck's remarks to him after one of his teams had traveled to Athens only to return to Atlanta with their tail between their legs after being drubbed 8 – 1 by the University of Georgia. Coach Aleck asked Crenshaw what the score had been, but rather than mention the score, Crenshaw expounded on the fine virtues of the contest. When Coach Aleck persisted, Crenshaw finally answered: "Only 8 – 1."

"Only 8 – 1!" Coach Aleck's voice rose. "What do you mean only? Why, that's the equivalent of 56 – 7 in football, and I don't see anything fine about it."

That fall the University of Florida stomped Coach Aleck's Yellow Jackets by a score of 55 – 7. After the game, Coach Aleck sat on a bench inside the empty football stadium lamenting the game's outcome while pondering the fate of his team and his future as a head football coach. Perhaps he should have become a doctor.

That's when Crenshaw appeared from nowhere to enjoy a hearty chuckle at Coach Aleck's expense.

"Ha, ha! Only 55 – 7," Crenshaw teased. "That's like 8 – 1 in lacrosse. It was a fine game and everybody had a good time. Ha, ha, ha!"

Coach Aleck managed to see the humor in the situation.

"I had it coming to me," he said.

Despite the dire outcome of the 1930 season, Coach Aleck had the good fortune of uncovering a jewel at the University of Tennessee thanks to a botched scouting trip.

2

Bobby Dodd and Years of Losing

Robert Lee "Bobby" Dodd had a flare for the dramatic, and above all else, he had luck on his side. Those who knew him or played against him swore he was the luckiest man on the planet. "Think you're lucky and you will be," Dodd always said. In later years this myth would grow until "Dodd's luck" became known to all in the college football world.

Georgia coach Wally Butts said, "If Bobby Dodd were trapped at the center of an H-bomb explosion, he would walk away with his pockets full of marketable uranium."

Dodd was born November 11, 1908, in Galax, Virginia, where the joke was that you could add a "y" to Galax and you'd still have a scruffy mountain town in southwest Virginia. His family moved to Kingsport, Tennessee, prior to his high school years, and Dodd's first play on a football field in 1924 as a Kingsport High freshman foreshadowed the luck that would follow him throughout his years. Weighing just 90 pounds, Dodd entered the game by slipping unnoticed from the sidelines to dart up the field and catch a long pass from the quarterback, his brother, John. According to legend, the trick play caused a free-for-all.

Dodd won the starting quarterback job from his brother the following season and began a successful reign as a single-wing quarterback. By his senior season his body had filled out to 160 pounds and he had developed into a top-notch quarterback with a keen football intellect and an uncanny talent for kicking the football. Only when Dodd's high school career drew to a close did he begin to think about his future. Though he had never displayed the same zest for studies that he had for football, he asked John, who had moved on to attend Georgia Tech, about his prospects for earning a football scholarship there. "I hate to hurt your feelings, Bobby," John replied, "but you're too damn dumb to go to Tech."

Dodd eventually accepted a scholarship to the University of Tennessee, where he played for General Robert Neyland, the legendary coach who was considered the dean of college football at the time. He remained an unmotivated student, but he earned nine letters in three sports at Tennessee—football, basketball, and baseball—while perpetuating the idea that a horseshoe must be permanently tucked in his back pocket.

Dodd's luck, real or perceived, stemmed in large measure from the confident manner in which he conducted himself. When Neyland coached the South team for the first North-South All-Star Game played in Atlanta, Dodd had a spot on the South team, affording Neyland the opportunity to call on his star player to give the team a lesson on how to punt the ball out of bounds. Reacting like an obedient student, Dodd asked Neyland where he wanted him to land the ball. Neyland threw his hat down along the sideline and told him "right about there." Dodd punted, and the ball landed on top of the hat. He then inquired of Neyland, "That about it, coach?"

Neyland suppressed a smile and played along with Dodd while the rest of the team shook their heads in disbelief.

Dodd became an All-American quarterback at Tennessee, leading the Volunteers to a 27 – 1 – 2 mark during the three seasons he started. He achieved his success through athletic ability, guile, and his unbounded confidence, which even extended to substituting his own plays for the ones Neyland sent in from the sidelines. "Dodd would run plays he made up in the huddle and then look toward the Tennessee bench and laugh," Neyland said later.

Dodd had the football IQ of a top coach. He could see the pieces of the puzzle and how they would fit together to trick a defense or gain an offensive advantage for a successful play.

In a game against Alabama in 1929, Tennessee was clinging to a slim lead when they took over on their own 6-inch line with a minute left to play. Rather than bang the ball against a solid wall of Alabama defenders on the first play, Dodd took the snap, moved around in the backfield to burn time from the clock, then threw out of bounds to incur an intentional grounding call. Today such a play would earn a safety call by the officials, but safeties were not awarded for such an infraction in 1929, so the penalty merely backed up the Volunteers half the distance to the goal line, or 3 inches.

Dodd repeated the strategy on second down, and once again the penalty moved the ball back half the distance to the goal—this time 1 ½ inches.

Displaying the nerves of a tightrope walker, Dodd then quick-kicked on third down, pushing Alabama back to the Tennessee 45-yard line, from where they had time for two frantic plays before the clock expired, making Tennessee the winner.

By the completion of Dodd's eligibility after the 1930 season, Tennessee fans had come up with the motto, "In Dodd we trust."

Word of Dodd's football intellect began to spread.

In advance of Georgia Tech's November 30, 1930 contest against North Carolina, Coach Aleck dispatched his line coach, Mack Tharpe, to Knoxville to scout North Carolina's game against Tennessee. Car problems caused Tharpe to miss the game, leaving the assistant with an empty notebook on the Tar Heels. In later years there would be any number of sources for scouting information, making the available knowledge on any team immense, but that was far from true in 1930. Tharpe knew that Tech would have to wing it against North Carolina without his report. Faced with such a prospect, he swallowed his pride and paid a visit to the Vols' locker room to ask Neyland for help. The Tennessee coach quickly pointed him in Dodd's direction, and Dodd talked while Tharpe listened. Upon returning to Atlanta, Tharpe told Coach Aleck, "Dodd's analysis of Carolina is better than any scouting report I could have made."

Tharpe did not forget Dodd's assessment when Tech had a vacancy for a backfield coach at the end of the 1930 season. Tharpe repeatedly touted Dodd for the position until Coach Aleck gave in to his line coach's persistence and invited Dodd to Atlanta to interview for the job.

History has blurred exactly what happened next. One account reported that Tech signed Dodd as an assistant coach on December 28, 1930, paying him a salary of $300 a month along with a $600 bonus if he showed up in Atlanta in time for spring football practice. Another story suggests a more covert departure from Tennessee. According to that account, Dodd traveled to Atlanta in the spring with the Tennessee basketball team for the Southern Conference basketball tournament, and when the team made its return to Knoxville, Dodd remained in Atlanta—just in time for spring football practice.

The only certainty is that Dodd accepted a position at Georgia Tech.

Others besides Coach Aleck and Tharpe recognized Dodd's potential. Among those wanting to accommodate Dodd's move from the playing field to the sideline were Neyland and Wallace Wade, the Duke coach. Instead, Dodd slipped into Atlanta like a burglar to begin his career at Tech, a move that infuriated Neyland.

Dodd's easygoing manner and sense of humor were apparent when he negotiated his contract with Tech. After being in Atlanta for several days, Dodd told the Tech athletic board that with so many pretty girls in the city, he needed to be paid more. That's how Dodd received a raise before he ever signed a contract to coach at Georgia Tech.

. . . . .

Dodd's satisfaction upon taking the position turned into a churning stomach when he got his first glance at the Tech team he would help coach.

"Our third-string boys at Tennessee were better than the best at Tech," Dodd said later. "Nobody but Coach Aleck could have gotten anything out of them."

Dodd liked to win, a trait honed under Neyland. He had also taken to heart the precision that played such a large part in Neyland's attack. Dodd never tired of recounting Neyland's preparation for Tennessee's game against Vanderbilt in 1929. One play called for Dodd to fake a handoff to a running back hitting the middle of the line, following which, amid the chaos, Dodd was to remain hunched over, hiding the ball in his lap. While the defense piled on the back, he was to slip nonchalantly out of the picture and then, upon reaching daylight, sprint for the goal line. In discussing the play's possible effectiveness with his coach, Dodd estimated that he could score from the 50-yard line, but Neyland factored his quarterback's speed against the probable elapsed time before the defense would recognize the fake and told Dodd that he could score from 20 yards out at most. Dodd privately disagreed with Neyland but respected his coach's judgment. As the game unfolded, he waited until he had driven his team to the Vanderbilt 20 before making the call. Everything unfolded just as it had in practice—the defense bit, allowing Dodd to scoot around the end before making an all-out sprint for the end zone. Although he scored a touchdown, he got tackled at the goal line, after precisely 20 yards.

"The General had it figured to the yard, and just sort of winked at me after the game was over," Dodd said.

Though Dodd possessed a great and innovative football mind, there were initial concerns about him as a coach because of his tendency to run around with players on the team. But that was before he met Alice Davis, one of the pretty Atlanta girls he had talked about, who was the sister of Tech halfback Wink Davis. After a short courtship, Dodd married Alice, which no doubt eased any skepticism about the pitfalls blocking his path toward becoming a fine coach. He continued to mature on the job, providing a nice counter presence to Coach Aleck. Dodd also coached the Tech baseball team and helped coach the basketball team. Tech athletes embraced him, and he enjoyed great popularity.

According to Shorty Roberts, a Tech quarterback in the early 1930s, Dodd "was the kind of man who would give you a lift just when you were feeling your lowest."

Despite Dodd's personality, his football pedigree, and his thirst for winning, Tech remained in a funk after his arrival, experiencing just two winning seasons from 1931 through 1941. During that time, in 1933 – 34, Coach Aleck and Tech earned themselves a black eye where civil rights were concerned.

Football in the South was a white-only game then. Not only were blacks not allowed on Southern teams, teams from the South would often refuse to play a team with a black player or players. Understanding that Michigan would be fielding a black player, Willis Ward, when Tech played the Wolverines in Ann Arbor on October 20, 1934, Coach Aleck alerted Michigan by letter in 1933 that Tech would not play that game if Ward participated.

President George W. Bush brought up the episode at the National Cathedral while delivering a eulogy for President Gerald R. Ford on April 19, 2008. Bush said, "Long before [he] was known in Washington, Gerald Ford showed his character and his leadership. As a star football player for the University of Michigan, he came face to face with racial prejudice. When Georgia Tech came to Ann Arbor for a football game, one of Michigan's best players was an African-American student named Willis Ward.

"Georgia Tech said they would not take the field if a black man were allowed to play. Gerald Ford was furious at Georgia Tech for making the demand and at the University of Michigan for caving in. He agreed to play only after Willis Ward personally asked him to. The stand Gerald Ford took that day was never forgotten by his friend."

Atlanta Constitution columnist Ralph McGill reminded his readers during the week of the game in 1934 that Tech's demand was not unique and that other Southern teams had engaged in the practice, including Vanderbilt in 1922, 1923, and 1934 and Georgia in 1931. McGill concluded, "Until this time-honored custom is honored more in the breech than the observance, it might be well for Southern and Northern teams to avoid scheduling games when there are any possibilities of racial friction."

McGill later moved from the sports page to write about national affairs and won a Pulitzer Prize in 1959 for his editorial support of civil rights.

Ward did not play against Tech, but Michigan made a last-minute request that, since Ward played end, it would only be fair for Tech not to play its starting end Hoot Gibson. Tech honored the request, and Michigan won the game 9 – 2.

Tech coaching staff (from left to right): Mack Tharpe, William Alexander, and Bobby Dodd. Tharpe would later serve in World War II.

Tech's best season after Dodd's arrival came in 1939, when the team went 7 – 2 after posting a 6 – 0 mark in the Southeastern Conference to become SEC co-champions. They finished the season with an appearance in the Orange Bowl against heavily favored Missouri. Dodd's influence on Tech's fortunes never shone brighter than that 1939 season. Though Coach Aleck remained the head coach, he concentrated mostly on defense while the offensive chores went Dodd's way.

Missouri had All-American quarterback Paul Cristman, whom many believed to be college football's best passer. When Cristman passed the Big Six champions to an early 7 – 0 lead, most figured the rout had begun. But Dodd and Coach Aleck knew one undisputable truth, which was that nobody had stopped the Tech offense all season.

Dodd and Coach Aleck had devised what football experts called the "hidden ball" offense. Like mad scientists, they had mixed a little of this with a little of that during the 1937 and 1938 seasons—recombining bits and pieces of plays and formations with new and different wrinkles—to come up with the concoction they unveiled in 1939. The end product was an offense based on deception, timing, and precision blocking.

Despite Tech's consistent offensive success in 1939, the experts believed that Missouri's bigger line would shut them down. But the Tigers could not stop what they could not see. The confusion created by the Tech offense was so effective that it caused a veteran radio announcer to completely miscall one after another in a succession of plays; he finally resorted to a self-imposed delay in calling the action when Tech had the ball.

Tech stormed from behind to beat Missouri 21 – 7, and Tech's stock went up with the win, which was considered a huge upset. Imitation is the sincerest form of flattery, and many in the coaching profession flocked to Atlanta after Tech's Orange Bowl win to study Tech game films, trying to fathom how to use an attack built on double and sometimes triple laterals and passes.

"I still can't figure out where they hid that ball," Cristman would say whenever asked about that Orange Bowl encounter against Tech.

Alas, an offensive scheme can do only so much to determine the outcome of a game. The players have to do the rest, and Tech did not have the players to do much winning in the years that followed; the team struggled to 3 – 7 and 3 – 6 records in 1940 and 1941. Dodd later commented about those years at Tech, saying, "No one else could have commanded the support of school, public, and players as Coach Aleck did while losing so many games. We had some good football players, but not great ones, during those lean years. Or not enough great ones."

Tech's problem stemmed partly from the difficulty of enrolling top-tier athletes in a technical institute. Some students are blessed with unusual academic prowess and others with rarefied athletic skills, but rare indeed is the well-rounded student athlete Tech needed to find. Further hurting the school's ability to enroll top athletes was the transfer of its Commerce Department to the University of Athens in 1933, which deprived it of courses that required far less attainment in higher mathematics and the sciences. Football players, like all members of the student body, were required to pass their courses in order to remain in school, much less play football. The increasingly narrow technical curriculum ensured that many athletes would either never set foot on the Tech campus or wouldn't remain there. To Coach Aleck's credit, he never bellyached about the hand he had been dealt. He steadfastly believed that being well rounded meant earning a rigorous education as well as participating in athletics.

During those lean years, America experienced the Great Depression, and Coach Aleck served as more than a football coach, helping to support the Tech athletic program with his own money. Mud River lived in Coach Aleck's heart, and he maintained a firm commitment to equality for others. When the coaches or trainers were not paid, Coach Aleck often stepped in to help out. Teaching ran through his blood, and throughout his tenure he retained a keen interest in developing student life and school spirit on the Tech campus. He even helped found the Ramblin' Reck Club (the "W" having been dropped from Wreck) in 1930—then known as the Yellow Jacket Cheering Club—to help promote school spirit and pride during a trying time.

Coach Aleck remained a bachelor until 1935, when, at the age of 46, he married Marie MacIntyre Scott, a widow with four children. Of his domestic life we have only this amusing flash: Coach Aleck walked to the breakfast table early one morning to eat by himself, and the cook asked him what he wanted. He responded, "I'll eat the rest of that barbecue hash we had last night. Just heat it up a little and put it on toast."

Coach Aleck wolfed down the barbecue and had just begun to sip his second cup of coffee when Mrs. Alexander appeared to tell him he had just eaten dogfood, not barbecue. Coach Aleck considered this and said, "Well, it was a little flat, but not bad."

* * * * *

Coach Aleck continued to nurture Dodd's growth and allowed Dodd autonomy, but Dodd never lost sight of who ran the show. He could see that his boss was a dominating man, and he understood that the boss needed to be in charge. Dodd also took note of how effective Coach Aleck was at handling players, coaches, alumni, and administrators.

William Alexander succeeded John Heisman as the head football coach at Georgia Tech, bringing a different, but also successful, style to the position.

Dodd flourished as an assistant at Tech, which didn't go unnoticed by other programs. Had Dodd coached in the later part of the century, it's extremely unlikely he would have remained at Georgia Tech as long as he did. The large contracts given to college football head coaches have brought with them high turnover due to the higher expectations. Sooner than later, coaches of Bobby Dodd's caliber are recruited for prestigious jobs paying big money. Vacancies were not as common in the 1930s and 1940s, but plenty of colleges would have loved to pry away him away from Tech, and he began to yearn for his own ship to steer.

Following Tech's splendid 1939 season, the University of Florida began courting Dodd to become their head coach. Dodd went to Gainesville in March 1940, and Florida officials wooed and flattered him, telling him what they thought he could do for their program. Having Dodd's luck in their corner appeared to be an attractive option for the Gators, who had never yet enjoyed football success. Clearly Dodd had the necessary acumen to be a successful head coach. Dodd, for his part, liked Florida's potential, and the job had many attractive perks. By March 28 he told his suitors that he wanted the job if they could offer him a good salary, a sufficient budget to hire high-caliber assistants, and a competitive number of football scholarships to hand out.

Dodd wanted a five-year deal but would have settled for three. He figured if he couldn't start winning in three years, Florida wouldn't want him around and he wouldn't want to remain there. All that separated him from leaving Tech for Florida was his signature on a dotted line—and informing Coach Aleck of his decision.

Dodd told Florida officials he wanted the job, but when he went to inform Coach Aleck, a pivotal conversation ensued.

"I'm going to Florida," Dodd told his mentor.

In the past when such offers had been directed Dodd's way, Alexander had adopted a fatherly tone, advising his understudy not to take the job because, in the long run, he'd be better off at Tech. Perhaps Coach Aleck took the Florida offer more seriously, or maybe he'd been pondering his own future, or maybe he just figured it was time to change tacks. He glared at Dodd through his steely blue eyes and barked, "The hell you are. Your place is at Georgia Tech. Now, get out of my office."

Dodd turned down Florida's offer, but not solely out of respect for Coach Alec. The head coach, it turned out, had been doing some maneuvering of his own.

Like everybody in the Tech family, Coach Aleck knew that Dodd would be his successor. He also knew he had aged and that having Dodd alongside him enhanced the chances of Tech returning to college football's center stage. The wily old coach wasn't about to let Tech's present and future go up in smoke without hedging his bets. While Dodd had been in Gainesville, Coach Aleck had recruited Dodd's wife, Alice, as his accomplice in a grand scheme to retain his talented head coach-in-training.

Coach Aleck knew how to handle money. He could maneuver a financial statement like a Wall Street wizard and could recognize the difference between a good investment and a ruse. Good values easily caught his attention. Several people who knew Coach Aleck suggested that, had he not been a football coach, he could have made millions investing, but the coach simply wasn't wired that way. His loyalties were to Georgia Tech, and his financial prowess was used only in the service of his alma mater and employer. That certainly included keeping Dodd in the fold.

Coach Aleck and Alice Dodd had taken a little excursion down Polo Drive and arranged to buy a house just across the street from the Ansley Golf Club. The coach had spotted the house and recognized its value immediately. When Dodd found out what Coach Aleck and his wife had done, Alexander told Dodd that the house would cost $4,800—hardly modest for the time—and would require a certain amount of money for a down payment, but the monthly mortgage payments would be no higher than paying rent.

"It's a pretty and well-built house," Coach Aleck told Dodd. "I've looked it over. It's in a good neighborhood. Go and close the deal. You'll never regret it."

Dodd put another $1,200 into renovations and just like that, the Dodd family had grown roots in Atlanta, and all was well with Tech football.

3

Boys' High and
Shorty Doyal

For more than three decades, beginning in 1912 and ending with the restructuring of the Atlanta school system after the 1946 game, Boys' High and Tech High waged a fierce rivalry from the same building in the city of Atlanta.

By 1940 the annual football game between the two schools reigned as the second biggest sporting event in the state of Georgia after the annual Georgia – Georgia Tech football game. Boys' High – Tech High games regularly outdrew Georgia Tech home games and University of Georgia games in Athens, just up the road. Crowds in excess of 20,000 were not uncommon. Professional football had not yet reached the South, and while professional baseball had, the major leagues had not.

Because segregation still reigned, all of the students at both schools were white males, many of whom arrived at school each day via Atlanta's streetcars. After boarding near their homes, students could get off at Whitehall or Alabama street or at Peachtree and Ellis streets, where "specials" waited to take them to their exit along Boulevard—or Monroe Drive, as it is known today—on the east side of the schools' property in time to begin classes at 8 A.M. Streetcars would be waiting for students on Boulevard after school at 2 o'clock. Atlanta covered just 37 square miles at that time; not until 1952 would the city expand to its current dimensions of 128 square miles.

Boys' High featured a liberal arts curriculum, and Tech High was focused on science and engineering. In a quirky arrangement, the two schools were housed in a single brick building facing Tenth Street and Piedmont Park. To accommodate the vast enrollment, portable wooden classrooms from World War I were deployed on the grounds and allocated to the two schools, with Boys' High's portables on the west side of the school along Charles Allen Drive and Tech High's on the east side along Boulevard. Potbelly stoves heated the portables in the winter, and open windows cooled them in the spring. The two schools' football teams even practiced at Piedmont Park at the same times, though at opposite ends of the park.

Other than Boys' High and Tech High, Atlanta had Marist High, a Catholic school, and Commercial High, a downtown school. "And if you didn't go to one of those you didn't go to school, that was it," said Phillip Maffett, who graduated from Boys' High in 1941. "So we got the cream of the crop at Boys' High and Tech High. That was where all the boys went. We pretty much dominated in all the sports, but particularly in football."

Every fall before the annual football game, the animosity between the two schools reached a fever pitch, spilling out of the big brick building to extracurricular shenanigans that included rock battles between rival groups of students. An incident involving a flagpole perhaps best exemplified the extent of the rivalry.

An American flag flew from a flagpole in front of the building that housed both schools. One year, just prior to the annual game, several Tech High students executed what appeared to be a perfect plan when they snuck onto the school grounds after dark and successfully raised a metal flag touting Tech High to a position just under the American flag. To make sure the flag would continue to fly, the students greased the flagpole so nobody could take down the newly positioned standard—or so they thought. The following day a Boys' High student drove by the flagpole, rose from a rumble seat, and emptied a 12-gauge shotgun into the metal flag, which fell to the ground. What remains of that flag can still be seen today at the Atlanta History Center.

The Tech High Smithies and the Boys' High Purple Hurricanes usually met at the end of the season, playing on a Friday night at Ponce de Leon Park, home of the minor league Atlanta Crackers baseball team. Most seasons saw the winner of the game advance to the Georgia Interscholastic Athletic Association (G.I.A.A.) state championship. Tickets for the contest were harder to come by than any other ticket in the state, and the game itself always exceeded available seating capacity to such an extent that a fire marshal could have issued as many citations as he cared to write. In addition to sitting in the grandstands or bleachers, fans climbed on top of parked freight cars on the railroad tracks just past the center field fence. When the game concluded, the victorious team and its fans would move to Ponce de Leon Avenue to begin a celebration march with police escort toward The Varsity, a drive-in restaurant located on North Avenue. On many occasions these parades were punctuated by altercations with the losing school.

The Varsity served as a hub for student activity. The self-proclaimed "World's Largest Drive-In Restaurant" stretched from Spring Street to the Georgia Tech campus; this was before an interstate highway cut through the middle of Atlanta. According to legend, Frank Gordy opened the restaurant in 1928 after dropping out of Georgia Tech at the urging of a professor, who had told him that a student with his grades should "quit and open a hot dog stand." The place became an Atlanta institution. In the early days of The Varsity, customers would pull into the large parking lot and a carhop would jump onto the car's running board to recite the menu, which consisted largely of chili dogs, hamburgers, fried onion rings, and an orange sherbet milkshake known as a "frosted orange."

Boys' High won championships in many sports, but football reigned supreme. Boys' High games were covered by the Atlanta newspapers as fulsomely as pro sports would be covered years later.

R.L. "Shorty" Doyal, who coached the Boys' High football team, was an icon on the campus and in the minds of Atlanta sports fans. His nickname served as a humorous contradiction to his actual stature. The man stood six-foot-five and towered over most of his football players on the practice field and students in the classroom, where he taught history. None of Doyal's students or players addressed this bigger-than-life man as "Coach." Rather, he was "Mister."

Doyal played football at Tech High and graduated in 1918 before heading across town to play for John Heisman at Georgia Tech, where he started as a lineman in 1919. After playing sparingly in 1920 due to illness, Doyal opted to go to work rather than play in 1921, according to an account from *The Atlanta Constitution*. He earned a bachelor of science in textiles engineering in 1922 and went to work at Tech High, where he became an assistant football coach.

Doyal remained at Tech High for three years before heading next door to Boys' High in 1925 to teach and coach. All told, he coached six sports, including boxing and fencing.

Boys' High's football success sprang from many factors, according to H.M. Furchgott, a Boys' High lineman who graduated in 1942 and went on to play at Georgia Tech.

"It was preparation, the coaching, the discipline, and the attitude that we had," Furchgott said. "But it was primarily Shorty Doyal. He was a great leader, a great disciplinarian. We wouldn't dare step out of line. We almost worshipped him. He had a brilliant football mind. He could have been a college coach at any college in the country. And many of us who went on to play in college thought he was as good as any of the college coaches we had. My brother, Charlie, played at Georgia, where Wally Butts was the head coach, and I played for Coach Alexander and Bobby Dodd. And we always thought Shorty Doyal was equal to all of them."

Boys' High played teams beyond the Atlanta area and even beyond Georgia. Their schedule always included an array of teams throughout the Southeast, which could mean road trips to Mississippi, Kentucky, North Carolina, and Florida.

Film study had not yet become a coaching staple during the first half of the twentieth century, but Doyal embraced it as a means of becoming a better and more successful coach. He even got reports from scouts who watched the NFL's Washington Redskins and New York Giants. Their reports and insights opened his eyes to using other formations, defenses, and techniques.

"We had at Boys' High a defense that would feature a six-, five-, or four-man front," Furchgott said. "In those days we didn't play anybody who did anything other than a 6-2-2-1 defense, but at Boys' High we had various defenses. Offensively, we always came out in the T-formation and then we'd shift to either the Notre Dame Box or a short punt formation. When we were in the box formation, the quarterback became a blocking back."

An offshoot of the single-wing formation that retained the single-wing's long snap, the Notre Dame Box featured a balanced line (unlike the single-wing), and the halfback shifted in from the "wingback" position to line up closer to the quarterback, fullback, and tailback, giving the backfield a box-like configuration. The balance of the formation made the direction of the play more difficult for the defense to predict, and the offense could more easily run to the "weak" side—i.e., the side opposite of where the tight end lined up.

In the single-wing the quarterback primarily blocked, whereas in the Notre Dame Box, the quarterback became a potential passer because he lined up where he could take a direct snap from the center. Deception and frequent shifts by the backs were key elements to the offense.

A single-wing tailback received a direct snap and carried the ball 90 percent of the time while also doing the passing. Passing from the single-wing usually involved the tailback sweeping to one side or the other before pulling back to pass. Tailbacks rarely dropped back to throw as quarterbacks do in modern passing offenses. All of the action in the single-wing started from a direct long snap. The Box would see the offense line up in a T-formation—which features the quarterback taking the snap from center and three running backs lined up behind the quarterback and parallel with the line of scrimmage—and shifting to the Box, which had a wingback, a blocking back, a fullback, and a tailback. The blocking back would line up by the right guard and direct his hands toward the center so he could occasionally take a snap directed his way. There weren't a lot of differences between the Notre Dame Box and the single-wing.

For many teams, the choice between running the two offenses came down to personnel. Teams with a "triple-threat" back—a tailback who could run, throw, and kick the football—usually employed the single-wing, while teams lacking that one outstanding player went for the diversity of the box.

Doyal understood the X's and O's of football, and he stood well ahead of his time in his emphasis on conditioning. He surmised that riding bicycles would help prevent knee injuries, and he also prescribed mountain climbing. He may have been wrong on the specifics—these offbeat activities did little to prevent knee injuries—but his cross-training suggestions strengthened the core muscles of the body—the thighs, hamstrings, abdominals, and quadriceps—which are generally acknowledged as the critical muscles for success in athletics. His ideas contrasted strongly with the prevailing wisdom, which discounted sports conditioning and pooh-poohed weightlifting as liable to make an athlete "too musclebound."

For all of Shorty Doyal's greatness, the most critical piece for Boys' High's success escaped from Furchgott's lips almost as an afterthought: "And also, Shorty Doyal knew how to get talent. This is amazing. He recruited high school players from the suburbs of Atlanta."

One can just imagine how Doyal's aura and winning ways attracted talented players toward Boys' High. Who wouldn't want to play for a living legend?

The regulations governing high school sports were sketchy and not nearly as stringent during Shorty Doyal's era. For example, Furchgott's brother, Charlie, was three years older than Furchgott yet continued to play at Boys' High because the rules allowed a player to be eligible through the age of 21. Doyal wasn't above suggesting to his players that they remain in school another year or two to better their chances of getting a college scholarship offer.

By the late 1930s, Doyal had been around the game most of his life and could recognize talent almost at a glance. Coaches like Doyal always dream of the day when a natural, the most perfect player conceived, seemingly falls from the sky like some figure from Greek mythology to grace their program. Many coaches never get that chance to capture lightning in a bottle, but Shorty Doyal was more fortunate. He realized his dream in 1937.

4

A Local Talent

Clinton Dillard Castleberry, Jr., was born in Atlanta on October 10, 1923. His father, Clinton Dillard, Sr., worked his way up from the bottom rung of the Atlantic Ice and Coal Company to eventually become its president. Clint Sr. hailed from Lumpkin, Georgia, and his mother was from Columbus, Georgia. Clint's great, great, grandfather had been a first cousin of James Oglethorpe, a British general and the founder of the colony of Georgia.

Clint Sr. maintained a neat appearance and exuded polish, from his manicured nails to his immaculate dress. His job required him to move his family to Americus for two years and Augusta for six before returning to Atlanta, where Clint spent most of his life.

The Castleberry house stood on Greenwood Avenue, a tree-lined street of brick homes that runs east and west between Highland Avenue and Ponce de Leon Place in the Virginia Highlands area of Atlanta. The Castleberry home's backyard, like neighboring yards on the south side of Greenwood, pitched upward on the hill. Some of Clint Jr.'s earliest memories were of shooting marbles "for keeps" with friends in his Georgia red clay backyard.

His reserved manner and even temperament were part of his makeup from early childhood. "He was a rather shy, quiet guy," said Phillip Maffett, who grew up in Castleberry's neighborhood and knew him from an early age. "He wasn't a loudmouth at all. He just was good at everything. Even back in grammar school, Clint was good in sports."

At a neighborhood park on East Ponce de Leon Avenue, the kids played all the sports, and Castleberry distinguished himself in every one of them. Even during games of Capture the Flag it became evident to all the neighborhood youths that Castleberry had special talents.

"When we played Capture the Flag at night, he was hell to catch," Maffett said. "He was something else, really—just an amazing athlete."

Castleberry graduated from Samuel Inman Grammar School before heading to Bass Junior High in the Five Points area. That was also the year he joined a neighborhood football team known as the "Bone Benders."

"Defenses couldn't do anything with him," Maffett said. "Nobody could tackle him. He was not big at all. He probably didn't even weigh 130 pounds back then. He was so shifty. You could never get your hands on him."

Despite unchallenged success, Castleberry remained modest and appeared shy to those who didn't know him. "He wasn't shy around us," Maffett said. "But he could be somewhat shy around grownups when he was younger. He was just a regular guy. He was not a braggart, just very humble and modest."

Castleberry felt most at home at a ballgame. When he wasn't playing a sport, chances were he could be found watching sports or even working around sports at nearby Ponce de Leon Park, just west of the railroad tracks from his home. Babe Ruth had once belted an epic home run during an exhibition at the historic park; it had sailed into a majestic magnolia tree past the center field fence, some 500 feet from home plate. The park also served as the home park of the Southern Association's Atlanta Crackers, whom Castleberry worked for during summer days. A flat roof covering the grandstands offered Castleberry a splendid view of the action while he fielded foul balls, dutifully relaying them back to the field.

"If you went to the game, you'd usually see Clint up there on the roof," Maffett said.

Several stories exist about Shorty Doyal's discovery of Clint Castleberry. The most romantic of these has Castleberry playing baseball one afternoon on a field adjacent to the Boys' High football practice field. Someone in the baseball game hit a home run that carried onto the Boys' High field, and one of the Boys' High football players retrieved the ball and threw it back toward the baseball game. Shortly thereafter someone kicked a football into the baseball game, and it ended up at Castleberry's feet in center field. Doyal watched as the skinny kid nonchalantly picked up the ball with his left hand and whistled a tight spiral back toward the football field. Size notwithstanding, Doyal recognized Castleberry's talent on the spot and shouted toward the baseball game, "Boy, come over here, what's your name?"

Everybody knew Shorty Doyal, so Castleberry obediently went to the coach and told him his name.

"You are now a football player," Doyal told him.

Another account has Doyal coaching a sandlot American Legion team, but more than likely the true story lies in the fact that Doyal coached youth sports, including baseball, as well as six sports at Boys' High. Doyal had a pulse on the community in which he reigned, and there's a good chance he knew about Castleberry's prowess on the football field even before Castleberry suited up for the Bone Benders or played American Legion baseball. Word spread fast to Doyal's ears about any raw talent in the area. Mining that talent and cultivating it to his advantage played a major role in Doyal's immense success.

Castleberry joined the Boys' High team as a sophomore in 1939 and made an immediate impact, though he still weighed just 129 pounds. In repose he looked like someone who had no business playing for a powerhouse football program, but in motion his true identity was revealed. Early in the season, his shifty moves made the difference in a Boys' High win against Savannah High School. He broke his arm prior to the game against Tech High, casting a pall over Boys' High's chances, but the team was talented enough to finish the 1939 season as undefeated Georgia state champions. Castleberry returned to practice prior to Boys' High's season-ending 26 – 0 loss to Miami High at the Orange Bowl, but he did not play in that game, which determined the Southern Prep Football Championship.

Critical to Miami High's win was the ball-carrying of David Eldredge, a 141-pound running back who scored three touchdowns and was clearly the best player on the field that day—a fact well noted by Doyal. The coach immediately got back to the drawing board looking for ways to improve his team for the next season.

Eldredge helped reaffirm Doyal's belief that coaching could take a team only so far. All the X's and O's in the world would not have stopped the talented Miami High back that night in the Orange Bowl. Talent had been the separating factor in the big game, which told Doyal that despite being a dominating state champion football team, Boys' High simply needed more talent—particularly if he wanted to be competitive in big interstate rivalries like the one against Miami High. After Christmas, Doyal put in place a plan to help find hidden Boys' High talent: interclass football.

Interclass games had once been a staple at Atlanta high schools but had fallen by the wayside. Now Doyal revived the practice at Boys' High. Regular weekly games determined which four teams would meet in a single-elimination tournament, and the winner of the game between the number 1 and 4 teams would meet the winner of the game between the number 2 and 3 teams for the school championship. Doyal, along with coaches Dwight Keith and Bill Orgain, scouted the games for varsity talent.

The schedule lasted until March, which fed right into spring football practice. Members of the winning team were awarded miniature silver footballs, and outstanding players were invited by Doyal and company to participate in spring drills with the varsity football team. Few honors could rival a personal invitation to spring football practice from Shorty Doyal.

Under Doyal's direction, Castleberry became one of the coaches of the interclass teams, as did Ralph Kennerly, Al Berman, Charlie Furchgott, Kale Alexander, Bill Bailey, Hoyt Fincher, and "Pig" DeFreese, all players on the Boys' High varsity team.

In addition to schoolwork and coaching his interclass team, Castleberry played on the Purples' basketball team. He stood just five-foot-nine, but his opponents learned shortly after the opening tip that a height advantage meant nothing if they couldn't keep up with the man they were trying to guard. Using his quickness and ball-handling ability to his advantage, Castleberry started at guard. Today he'd be called a point guard, but such a designation did not exist then. A surviving photograph of Castleberry in a basketball uniform reveals the source of his quickness—a pair of hamstrings to rival those of Seabiscuit. He'd developed the muscles from playing sports his entire life, and they were the primary propulsion system for his elusiveness and speed.

Basketball eventually gave way to spring football, and Doyal, who had coached and seen many a fine player by this juncture, continued to marvel at the rocket in his backfield. After watching what would be his 1940 team beat a team of former Boys' High players, the "Past Purples," by a score of 7 – 0 in the spring, Doyal said Castleberry was better than Johnny Bosch, who had played at Georgia Military Academy High School before becoming a standout quarterback at Georgia Tech.

During the win by the 1940 team, Castleberry caught a pass from Hoyt Fincher and didn't stop running until he was in the end zone. According to Doyal's description of the run, the elusive Castleberry had gone to his right, gone to his left, and finally went back to the center of the field to score. Not prone to hyperbole, Doyal waved his arms excitedly while extolling Castleberry's many virtues to a reporter from *The Atlanta Constitution*.

"He's already a brilliant back," Doyal said. "True, he's flea-sized—around 138—but man he has it all!

"He can pass and he can catch 'em. He can run with, or away from, the best ones. And he's smart—one of the greatest safety men I've ever seen in football. Yessir, he'll be better than Jonny Bosch."

The game against the departing seniors and alumni ended Boys' High's formal spring practice in 1940, leaving Doyal to lament that there were rough edges that needed to be smoothed in order for the team to have a successful 1940 campaign. Doyal's moaning and lamenting fit the nature of the beast. Football coaches are perfectionists, never happy with what they have. The coach's mood visibly lightened, however, when he began to think out loud about Castleberry. "But if they all were like Castleberry. . . ."

Castleberry never seemed fazed by the many compliments he

received. He went about his business and lived simply, following the seasons. Fall meant football, winter basketball, and spring baseball. Once spring football was complete, he simply moved on to baseball season, where he played center field for the Purples, patrolling the open turf with ease.

While Castleberry had played an integral role in Boys' High's fortunes during 1939, he exploded during the 1940 season. Playing quarterback in Boys' High's Box formation, Castleberry kicked off the season by leading the team to a 19 – 0 win over Commercial High School in front of a crowd of 10,000 at Georgia Tech's Grant Field.

Marist was next on the schedule, which made for an interesting matchup since Castleberry's friend Joe Wasser played for Marist. During the summer, Wasser served as head foul ball man at Ponce de Leon Park, where Castleberry worked as his assistant. The two teams had played to a tie the previous season and appeared headed to another tie in 1940, since neither team had scored heading into the fourth quarter.

Late in the quarter, however, Castleberry lined up as the running back in a short punt formation to the right. After taking the snap, he executed a half spin, faked a handoff to fullback Alfred Berman, then broke off right tackle into a small clearing for what would have been a 10-yard gain. But Castleberry had the gift of being able to find calm in the chaos of bodies slamming against one another. To many the game moved too quickly, and they would panic and make poor decisions in the face of adversity. But Castleberry's understanding of the game and his athletic ability allowed the game to move slowly for him. Suddenly in the clear against Marist, he saw another option as it popped into his field of vision. Out of nowhere, he leaped high and whipped an overhead lateral across the field to where Bill Bailey stood in the flat. "Easy Bill" hauled in the pass and ran the remaining 25 yards into the end zone for the only score in a 7 – 0 Boys' High win before a crowd of 11,000 at Grant Field.

Off to a 6 – 0 start, Boys' High appeared unstoppable with Castleberry leading the way. He had already scored six touchdowns, which placed him behind Tech High's Jackie Pounds for the scoring lead, but Castleberry rarely played a complete game due to the lopsided nature of the Boys' High wins.

Heading into the annual game against Tech High, *The Atlanta Constitution* described Castleberry as "the slickest eel in football around these parts." He lived up to that description during a rain-soaked affair between the rivals at Grant Field, with 14,000 watching.

Sloppy field conditions helped fashion a scoreless tie after a half of football. The teams combined for five fumbles and just six first downs in the half, and Castleberry's banged-up left shoulder added to the Purples' woes. Unknown to the Tech High Smithies, he could not have fired a pass if he had wanted to—but the threat of a Castleberry pass could be equally as dangerous as a pass itself. With Boys' High on the Tech High 15 and facing a fourth and goal, everybody at Grant Field figured a pass from Castleberry to be the obvious play. Instead, he took the snap, faked into the line, then sprinted wide to the left side and beat the defense to the stripe for the first touchdown of the game. Boys' High went on to win the game 12 – 0 and cinch another G.I.A.A. championship. The Purples had not allowed opposing teams to score a single point in the 1940 season.

That changed the following week when the Purples traveled to Rome, Georgia, to play Rome High. The Hilltoppers blocked a punt that went out of the end zone for a safety. But Castleberry scored on runs of 15 and 11 yards, and Boys' High took a 13 – 2 win to remain undefeated. After a win in Knoxville, Tennessee, over the Knoxville High Trojans, the Purples prepared for their annual trip to Miami, hoping to avenge the previous year's loss.

Boys' High's football team traveled by train to away games, boarding at the Terminal Station. Transporting high school kids to overnight destinations is often a good way to court disaster, since the time away from home can tempt even the most obedient teenager to some kind of misbehavior. And that might have been the case with Boys' High had Shorty Doyal not been the coach. Nobody can say what the consequences of misbehaving on the train might have been, because nobody ever dared misbehave. Shorty Doyal commanded respect and carried an air of power. Testing him was simply out of the question for even the most boisterous teenagers.

"We wouldn't dare step out of line," M.H. Furchgott said. "Coach Doyal wouldn't have put up with it. We almost worshiped him."

Doyal could be quirky in his own endearing way, too. He wore a derby to games for good luck, and he once went to great lengths on behalf of a cat that he felt brought Boys' High good luck. "Blackout" was a dark-colored cat that Doyal found in the gym prior to the start of the 1940 season. He boxed up the cat and kept her on the bench for early-season wins over Commercial and Marist before the cat disappeared in early September. Because Doyal regarded Blackout as a good-luck charm, he offered as a reward for the cat's return a deflated football and a broken baseball bat. The cat finally rolled back home to Doyal's house that November, but Blackout returned streetwise and wild, which made catching him difficult. Doyal figured he needed all the luck he could conjure up for Boys' High's coming trip to Miami to play Miami High, and Blackout had proven to be a talisman, so he declared his intention to work himself into better shape so he could chase down the good-luck kitty. Doyal initiated a series of foot races against his players after Thanksgiving dinner, including a race against Leerie Jenkins, one of the fastest players on the team. In a testament to Doyal's athleticism at age 41, he won all of the races that took place that day.

Excitement about traveling to Miami ran deeper than a train ride for the Boys' High squad. They would be playing before a large crowd in the Orange Bowl against a formidable team. Miami High's coach, Jess Yarborough, predicted that his Stingarees would defeat Boys' High by the score of 14 – 6, while other coaches from the Miami area also forecast a Boys' High defeat at the hands of the undefeated Stingarees. After all, Miami High had mopped the Orange Bowl with the squad from Atlanta the previous season. What they neglected to factor in was that Castleberry had still been recovering from a broken arm the previous year and had not been a part of the Purples' attack.

Yarborough irked Doyal and the Boys' High team with his remarks, which was nothing new for the Miami High coach. Even the mild-mannered Castleberry reacted to the lack of respect his team was getting. Precisely because his remarks before the team left Atlanta were so uncharacteristic of him, people listened when he told reporters to "go ahead and write your story now and say 'Boys' High stings Stingarees.'"

A smiling Claude Bond. The Georgia Tech trainer, who occasionally helped out at Boys' High, was said to be quick-witted and a source of great humor for the players.

To help treat and prevent injuries in the game, Boys' High borrowed Georgia Tech's trainer Claude Bond, which added a little personality to the trip. *The Atlanta Constitution* described him as "old Mother Bond," someone who "really knows how to keep her youngsters in line. The big fellow with the ready wit was for all the world like a mother bear slapping little baby bears away from the beehive."

Castleberry's words were prophetic, and his performance turned out to be the difference in the game. Throughout the game his punt returns prevented the Stingarees from boxing up the Boys' High offense, and his 30-yard touchdown reception put the game on ice in a 13 – 0 win that gave the Purples the Southern Championship.

The game against Miami High took place on December 6, 1940, and nobody on the field that night had any idea how dramatically their lives would change a year later.

The week following the Purples' epic victory in Miami, Boys' High finished the season by winning a game at Grant Field against a team of Atlanta-area high school all-stars. Once again Castleberry stood out, particularly with his punt returns, which, according to reports, "pleased the fans most" in a 14 – 6 Purples' win.

Despite Castleberry's heroics during the 1940 season, college scouts weren't convinced his game could move to the next level. The problem, they said, was his size. Frustrated after hearing such pronouncements on countless occasions, Doyal said of his star player, "He has the finest spirit and the best football temperament of any player I ever coached, and despite those 132 pounds he weighs he will run some of the big guys crazy in college. Just wait and see."

* * * * *

One couldn't overestimate the importance of sports in Castleberry's life, but he managed to find an outlet away from the athletic fields by spending time with Shirley Poole. Many of the high school courtships for Boys' High students involved girls who attended Girls' High, but Poole was an exception. She attended North Fulton High School, just outside Atlanta city limits, north of Castleberry's home.

"We started dating when we were 16," Poole said. "He was very sincere and had a cute personality. I was not even aware that he was a special football player when we started dating. I have no brothers and sisters and knew nothing about football or baseball. So the fact he played football, or any sport, didn't mean too much to me because I didn't realize that he was special. I could tell that he loved sports, though. He loved sports and he seemed to be more interested in sports than academics."

Castleberry liked that Poole wasn't enamored with him because of his athletic exploits. She rarely even attended his games.

Among the more popular activities for high school kids in Atlanta was going to The Varsity or attending the dances hosted by various high school sororities and fraternities. After dates or during the afternoons when they weren't playing sports, guys would often haunt the pool hall next to The Varsity.

A typical date for Castleberry and Poole consisted of driving "somewhere to get a Coca Cola."

"He had a car. It wasn't a new car, but he had an automobile," Poole remembered.

They didn't like to bowl or dance, though they did go roller-skating from time to time.

"He was very capable and able to do almost anything he tried," Poole said.

And there were plenty of movies to see, too.

"We both really liked the movies, so we went to a lot of them," Shirley said. "And we loved going to The Varsity."

She laughed, recalling the antics of the parking lot waiters at The Varsity.

"They would stand on the running boards and sing about hot dogs, hamburgers, and so forth," she said. "You never went inside."

A wonderful slice of Americana unfolded daily among the cliques and factions that huddled together in different pockets of The Varsity parking lot, visiting from one car to the next to catch up on the latest gossip or just socialize. Anytime Clint and Shirley went there, Shirley couldn't help but notice her boyfriend's standing among his peers. Girls wanted to be with him, and boys wanted to be like him.

"He was a very shy and sincere person—very modest," Poole said. "People were always telling him, 'You're the greatest football player we've ever had.' He didn't take compliments too well. He heard it all the time. I kind of liked hearing it. Naturally it was flattering."

Quiet moments away from the adoration were welcome, too, particularly for Clint, who often took Shirley home to spend time with his parents and his younger brother, Jimmy.

"His daddy and mother were very sweet people," Poole said. "Jimmy was three years younger. Even Jimmy idolized his brother. Clint was a good big brother. You could just tell everybody in the family was crazy about Clint. And Clint was very family oriented."

Typically, playing cards served many families as the primary form of entertainment in that day, but visits to the Castleberry home were different.

"Nobody ever played cards," Poole said. "I never got over that. You know how cards were the entertainment for a lot of families? At Clint's house it was always talking, talking. We'd talk about current events. I can remember his grandmother and grandfather being there. Clint called them 'Big Momma' and 'Big Papa.' Sometimes we'd go see them at their house, too. They lived in a small home in Atlanta. And he had an aunt and an uncle who lived in Decatur."

The couple also went to church together, frequenting the church Poole attended, Second Ponce de Leon Baptist on Peachtree Road.

"I couldn't have a date Saturday night if I didn't go to church on Sunday," Poole said.

Churchgoer, modest, and talented, Castleberry sounded like a too-good-to-be-true figure.

"Such a nice guy," M.H. Furchgott said. "I never, ever remember him using a cuss word. And when things got tough in the game and so forth, he never got downhearted. He was just an outstanding person, and always had great manners and showed respect for his teachers and elders."

But an aspect of his charm to those who knew him was the fact that he was a regular guy.

"And not a goody-good boy," Furchgott said. "I was one of two or three people on the team who didn't smoke; he would occasionally smoke like one of his contemporaries, but he always remained mild-mannered."

5

Boys' High Finale

By the fall of 1941, Castleberry had earned All-State honors in football, basketball, and baseball and had grown to a solid 152 pounds. With most of the 1940 Boys' High team returning, the Purples were favored to once again rule high school football in the South.

True to form, the Purples opened the 1941 season on a Thursday night at Grant Field by demolishing Commercial High 40 – 0. Castleberry had an electrifying 55-yard punt return for a touchdown during the rout. Next came a 46 – 0 romp over Marist that saw Castleberry catch one touchdown and run for another.

Charlie Roberts of *The Atlanta Constitution* described the Purples' third game of the season, against Jesup High in Jesup, Georgia, as follows:

"Jesup High last night was out of its class like Gypsy Rose Lee singing opera, and fell heir to a 58 – 0 lambasting at the hands of Boys' High's defending Southern champions."

Castleberry ran for an early 18-yard touchdown to start the Purples' scoring, then left the game minutes into the second half.

After five games, Boys' High had scored 198 points while holding their opponents scoreless, and the differential would have been far greater if not for Doyal's abhorrence of running up a score. Much to Castleberry's chagrin, the best way to keep the score down was to limit his playing time. He was the only Boys' High player to have scored as many as two touchdowns in one game, and he'd only done that twice. Still, he led the G.I.A.A. in scoring with 42 points.

In the midst of that glorious fall, the Boys' High student body elected Castleberry the school president. Meanwhile, Doyle, an advocate of well-rounded students, cited Castleberry and other athletes while touting the benefits of being a student-athlete. Somehow during the little time remaining to Doyle after coaching countless sports teams, teaching history, and caring for his family, he compiled the data and calculated that just 25 percent of the school's athletes from the previous school year had failed to pass all their subjects, while 50 percent of the entire student body had failed to pass. The student body as a whole had been absent from 8 percent of their classes, as opposed to 4 percent for student-athletes. And 26 percent of the student body found their names on the school's "black list"—indicating that they had failed to turn in books at the end of the year—while just 10 percent of the athletes were on the list. In short, Doyal believed that wearing a jock strap cured all ills for a high school student.

Castleberry's best friend from early childhood was Don Paschal. Their mothers were best friends, and the two boys grew up as constant companions and made a pact to attend the same college. Ironically, Paschal served as Castleberry's backup on the Boys' High team. Most would say that Paschal equaled Castleberry as a pass receiver and had almost equal skills in every other phase of the game. Paschal would have started for most high school teams in the country. But Boys' High had only one Clint Castleberry, and he kept his best friend on the bench, at least until Doyal saw victory at hand. (Sitting on the bench was taken literally in the 1940s. If a player wasn't in the game, he sat on the bench rather than crowding the sidelines. Even the coach might be seen sitting on the bench, sometimes smoking a cigar or cigarette while watching his team perform.)

Castleberry quickly found himself on the bench in Boys' High's 64 – 0 win over Georgia Military Academy on October 16, 1941.

He scored three touchdowns and had a 60-yard punt return for a fourth touchdown called back due to a penalty as the Purples extended their winning streak to 17 games. Castleberry played only a quarter against the Cadets yet retained the team scoring lead with 10 touchdowns in six games.

* * * * *

Bright and shining though that autumn was for Boys' High, a dark cloud loomed over the United States, casting a shadow on any young man eligible for military service. Adolph Hitler's invasion of Poland on September 1, 1939, had irrevocably ended British Prime Minister Neville Chamberlain's policy of appeasement, and two days later England and France had jointly declared war on Germany.

Despite the Axis invasion of France and air war against Britain, the Axis occupation of most of continental Europe, and the Tripartite Pact of September 1940 uniting Japan with Germany and Italy, isolationist tendencies still ruled America in the fall of 1941. With memories of World War I still fresh in the minds of most Americans, there was little appetite for direct military involvement. Still, President Roosevelt was taking what measures he could to support the Western Allies and China, directing supplies and materiel to Britain and embargoing trade with Japan. The United States Navy had begun a significant buildup following Germany's invasion of France in 1940, and the city of Atlanta felt like a part owner of a new cruiser, the USS *Atlanta*, which was christened on September 6, 1941, by *Gone with the Wind* author Margaret Mitchell during a launching ceremony at the Federal Shipbuilding and Drydock Company in Kearny, New Jersey.

By October, America's chances of avoiding the global conflagration seemed increasingly remote. The portents were everywhere, and another came on October 31, 1941, when German submarine U-562 torpedoed the USS *Reuben James*, which was engaged in convoy duty off the coast of Iceland. The four-stack Clemson-class destroyer earned the distinction of becoming the first U.S. Navy ship sunk in pre-World War II action. In the aftermath of that act of aggression, the country crept closer to the inevitable. The headline in the *London Daily Mail* read, "U.S. on the last mile into war."

Closer to home, an editorial in *The Atlanta Constitution* announced, "For the simple fact is, in the North Atlantic at least, we are at war with Nazi Germany."

Feelings of national pride began to swell within the young men who knew they would be the ones to carry the torch overseas once the inevitable became reality. Weeks later, a surprise attack on a U.S. naval base would vanquish American pacifism and push the nation into war. For the time being, however, football provided much-needed reassurance of a world that still made sense. And in Atlanta, there was no greater diversion for football fans than watching Clint Castleberry roll up and down the gridiron.

"The Comet" scored four touchdowns in a 45 – 0 win over Benedictine High in Savannah and two more in one quarter of work against Jordan High of Columbus, Georgia, to give him 16 touchdowns for the season. Paschal ranked third in scoring with eight touchdowns, which provided a good indication of how little Castleberry was allowed to play and why his statistics were not the best indication of what an outstanding player he was. Nobody returned punts like Castleberry. Once in the open field, his elusiveness made him nearly impossible to corral. He was a dangerous runner any time he carried the ball.

Castleberry had also evolved into a precise and accurate passer, all the more difficult to defend because he threw left-handed. Yet he didn't throw much because, in addition to being the best passer around, he was also the best receiver. As if all those talents were not enough to make any football coach fall in love with Clint Castleberry, he was also coachable and a natural leader, leading by example. His mere presence soothed. Knowing their team had the best player anywhere injected confidence into his teammates.

Ironically, good as he was, Castleberry hid a constant insecurity beneath a confident manner. "He was always afraid somebody was going to win his job, and he was forever tugging at my sleeves when I had him on the sidelines," Boys' High assistant Dwight Keith told *The Atlanta Constitution*. "He never thought he was very good. A lot of people don't recall, but Castleberry was a deadly defensive player, a sure tackler at safety. And that was another worry for him. He used to say, 'If they score on us, it will be my fault because I am the last man.'"

If the mighty mite of a football player doubted his own abilities, his lack of size may have been the reason. But Doyal entertained no such doubts. He knew what having Castleberry on his team meant and what an impact he had on a game. "I had to take him out to keep the score down," Doyal said.

Castleberry grew so frustrated at not getting to play during the Jordan game that he begged Doyal to let him back on the field.

"Please let me in there," Castleberry said. "Let me play guard. Let me play anywhere. I don't want to run with the ball. I want to play some."

Doyal wasn't about to bite, particularly with Tech High on deck as the Purple Hurricanes' next opponent. Castleberry would just have to bide his time and save his best effort for the annual rivalry game.

To that point of the season, Boys' High had totally outclassed their rival against common opponents, and many Georgia football fans that year concluded that Tech High did not belong on the same field with Boys' High. Doyal, however, refused to buy into the hype. Instead he stressed that football games weren't won by the number of inches of newspaper column space devoted to a team. Doyal had lived around this particular rivalry his entire life, and he knew well that strange things tended to happen whenever the two teams met. In the 1931 contest, for example, Tech High supposedly had the horses to run roughshod through Boys' High's eleven, but instead the Purple Hurricanes had come away with a 13 – 0 win, which was still considered the biggest upset in the history of the series.

Doyle reminded his team of that historical upset and its implications for their pending meeting. Tech High had nothing to lose, and their student body reflected that, raining rotten tomatoes and rocks on a Boys' High pep rally in the school's gym. Off campus, the city of Atlanta greeted the thirty-first meeting of the two teams with eager anticipation. A special radio broadcast on WATL, airing the night before the game, featured Doyal and Castleberry talking about the game.

By Saturday, Grant Field had the festive appearance of a gala event. The stands filled with a rich tapestry of Boys' High's purple and white and Tech High's blue and gold. By the 2:30 afternoon kickoff, the grandiose setting had convinced the Tech High faithful that, by the will of the football gods, there was some kind of magic at work, brewing up an upset.

Such pageantry has a way of slanting emotions and determining the momentum of a contest, particularly in rivalry games, but Boys' High didn't share the same vibe and quickly dispelled any notion that an upset might occur. The Purple Hurricanes took charge from the outset. Castleberry got roughed up early and did not play much, primarily due to a hurt knee. Nevertheless, Boys' High roared to a 45 – 0 win, claiming their third consecutive G.I.A.A. and city crowns in the process.

Furchgott would later remember that an interesting twist in the rules of the day had a dramatic effect on the 1941 rivalry game.

"When a passer threw the ball, he could potentially become a defensive player if he threw an interception," Furchgott said. "So after he threw the ball, he was fair game for any rushing lineman. We were told to body block their quarterback every time he threw the ball. We wore him out. Obviously, that rule was changed."

Boys' High's players received their reward the Wednesday after the game when they dined in the school cafeteria on a victory turkey luncheon accorded the winner of the annual rivalry. In typical Shorty Doyal style, the Purples' head coach donned his good luck derby while carving the turkey. After school that same day, the team caught a train for Mississippi to take on Meridian High, a team that had scored 382 points on the season and claimed to be national prep champions. Boys' High had tallied 398 points.

A banged-up Boys' High team arrived in Meridian with little sleep after the train ride from Atlanta to go against the local team in conditions that played to the strength of Meridian High's strong offensive and defensive lines. A mud-soaked Roy Stadium played host to the game, slowing down the speedy Purples. Castleberry and Paschal each scored a touchdown, but in the end, Boys' High had to block an extra point toward the conclusion of the game to come away with a 13 – 13 tie, thereby ending a 20-game winning streak during which no touchdowns had been scored against the Purples.

"The whole game was played in the rain," M.H. Furchgott said. "Oh my goodness, there must have been a half an inch of water on the field. Otherwise, I think we would have beaten them by a couple of touchdowns. They did have a very good team. We were fast and we were deceptive, which just didn't work that well in that kind of weather. That really slowed us down."

Boys' High returned home surprised and disappointed by the outcome, but they had to recover quickly to face the team from Hopkinsville, Kentucky, that was traveling to Atlanta to play them the following week at Ponce de Leon Park. Hopkinsville brought with them a 23-game winning streak, and all the pregame talk centered on the coming match-up between Castleberry and Tommy Gray, Hopkinsville's running back, who had scored 216 points during the season. While Gray had compiled an impressive point total, everyone in the Purple Hurricane camp noted that Castleberry had scored 108 points while averaging little more than a quarter of playing time per game.

No questions remained after the game regarding who was the better player. Castleberry ran for one touchdown on a fake pass, caught two touchdowns, and threw another, while Gray, who was known as "The Gray Streak in the Blue Grass," was completely shut down during a 47 – 0 Boys' High win

* * * * *

The list of colleges interested in Castleberry began to grow. Included in the mix of approximately nine were Georgia Tech, Georgia, and even Army, a national power at the time.

Miami High coach Jess Yarborough watched the Hopkinsville rout from the stands, as Boys' High would be the Stingarees' next opponent the following week at the Orange Bowl. While scouting, Yarborough also managed to make several comments of a similar flavor to those he'd made in advance of the previous season's game. He told reporters he wasn't too impressed by Boys' High, and went so far as to say there would be plenty of action on the game and that the bettors had the Stingarees as solid 6-point favorites. In Yarborough's defense, Miami did appear to have an edge. The Stingarees had beaten Savannah High 34 – 0, while Boys' High had beaten them just 12 – 0. And although Miami and Boys' High had beaten Lanier High by similar scores—45 – 0 and 42 – 0, respectively—Lanier coaches Stooge Davis and Tom Porter gave the Purples only an outside chance versus Miami. Yarborough felt he had the best team he'd ever coached.

Twenty-seven players, the coaching staff, and miscellaneous other members of the Boys' High entourage boarded a special Central of Georgia train at Terminal Station and departed Atlanta at 10:05 on Tuesday morning, December 2, 1941. The team stopped in Jacksonville for Tuesday and Wednesday nights, rooming at the Casa Marine Hotel at Jacksonville Beach. After a morning swim in the Atlantic Ocean, the team went through a Wednesday afternoon workout.

"Jacksonville was the thrill of a lifetime for most of us, because we'd never seen the ocean," Furchgott said. "We practiced near a beach at a local high school, then we got to play on the beach. For a high school kid, that was something else."

The team traveled the final leg to Miami by train on Thursday, the day of the game, arriving approximately five hours before kickoff.

Bruce Smith and Arnold Tucker epitomized the talent level at Miami High. They would go on to become the starting quarterbacks for Army and Navy, respectively. Tucker would come to be known as "Chuckin' Tuck" because of his prowess passing the football for an Army team coached by legendary Earl Blaik that featured "Mr. Inside" and "Mr. Outside" – Doc Blanchard and Glenn Davis.

But Castleberry stole the show, electrifying the crowd of 15,944 on offense, defense, and punt returns all night, though he could never break completely loose. The Purples went up 7 – 0 in the second quarter and held the ball most of the final quarter without being able to put any additional points on the board. The two Southern powerhouses battled to the end like the champions they were, finishing in a 7- 7 tie. Afterward, Yarborough approached Castleberry and told him, "Son, if I ever see you again, it will be too soon."

Boys' High remained in Miami for the Friday night game between the University of Miami and Virginia Military Institute, then headed to Atlanta by train, arriving home on Saturday, December 6, 1941.

6

America at War

The day after Boys' High's return from Miami, Clint Castle-berry and Shirley Poole went to an afternoon movie at the Loew's Grand Theatre on Peachtree Street. *Gone with the Wind* had staged its much ballyhooed world premiere at that theater on the frigid evening of December 15, 1939, and spotlights positioned in front of the theater had shot across the sky while an estimated crowd of 300,000 lined the streets, hoping for a glimpse of Clark Gable or Vivien Leigh. When Clint and Shirley left the theater almost two years later, they experienced a bustle of activity of a different sort outside. Emotions were riding high. It was December 7, 1941.

"They were selling newspapers everywhere, yelling, 'Extra! Extra!' there on the street when we came out around four or five o'clock," Poole would remember years later. "There was a pretty good crowd there."

The Japanese had launched a sneak attack against the U.S. naval base at Pearl Harbor in a move designed to cripple the United States Navy Pacific Fleet. This devastating strike came as a complete surprise, given that high-level negotiations to prevent war were still underway, but in fact those negotiations were drawing to an unsuccessful end, making war in the Pacific an increasingly likely outcome.

Japan had invaded Manchuria in 1931, had begun a full-scale military buildup in 1934, and had been engaged in war with China since invading that country in 1937. In an effort to end the aggression, President Franklin D. Roosevelt had relocated the Pacific Fleet to Pearl Harbor in 1939 and had progressively restricted exports of oil, iron, and steel to Japan, culminating in a full oil embargo as of July 1941. Japan depended on the U.S. for most of its oil and could not ignore the embargo.

On September 27, 1940, however, Japan had joined Germany and Italy in the Tripartite Pact, which committed all three so-called Axis Powers to a war against any one of them. Japan was now calculating that war in the Pacific would immediately involve America in the war in Europe, enabling Japan to expand its empire into Southeast Asia—the British colonies of Burma and Malaya and the Dutch East Indies—valuable sources of rubber, oil, and other resources. Crippling the U.S. Pacific Fleet and capturing U.S. bases in the Philippines were keys to the Japanese plan.

The Japanese Navy taxied six aircraft carriers to within striking distance of Pearl Harbor's shores. On board were approximately 353 deadly fighter planes loaded with torpedoes and bombs. Just before 8 A.M. Hawaiian time on December 7, the Japanese unleashed this force. The attack sank four U.S. battleships, damaged four more, and sank or heavily damaged three destroyers, three cruisers, and one minelayer. Approximately two hundred U.S. planes were destroyed without taking off, and more than 2,400 Americans were killed, while another 1,282 were wounded.

"It was a shock to everybody," Poole said. "All of us were trying to think of those we knew who were over there right then, wondering if they were alive, how many people were killed, that sort of thing. Clint knew people who were over there, and I knew several people's brothers who were in the service at that time."

On the following day, December 8, President Roosevelt appeared before a joint session of Congress while also addressing the American public via radio. In his speech, he called December 7 "a date that will live in infamy." Congress needed all of seven minutes to declare war against Japan.

On December 11, 1941, Germany and Italy responded by declaring war on the United States. Making the announcement at Reichstag in Berlin, German chancellor Adolf Hitler noted that war with the United States was unavoidable due to the Tripartite Agreement, but he also cited the healthy doses of economic and military aid the Soviet Union and United Kingdom were receiving from the United States. In addition, Hitler viewed the United States as an ideological enemy due to America's mixed racial composition, which, in his eyes, made the country inferior to Germany's Aryan race. Finally, he declared that forcing the United States to fight a war in two theaters would help ensure ultimate victory for the Axis Powers. Once that victory had been won, Germany, Italy, and Japan would work together to establish "a new and just order."

If the words of the German ruler weren't enough to send a chill through any American citizen, President Roosevelt's words to Congress did. Roosevelt stressed the urgent need of the free world to act against an enemy embracing savagery and barbarism. "The forces endeavoring to enslave the entire world now are moving towards this hemisphere," he said. "Delay invites danger."

Football suddenly took a back seat to world affairs for the Boys' High team and for youth all over the United States. Once-shining futures dimmed with uncertainty as the population of a nation rallied to confront the overt threat to its way of life. As young men flocked to sign up for military service, the future of sports in America was thrown into doubt.

· · · · ·

The Purples had one game remaining on their schedule—a game on New Year's Day, 1942, against an undefeated Lee Edwards High team from Asheville, North Carolina. The contest had been dubbed "The Milk Bowl" because the game, sponsored by the Atlanta Kiwanis, would benefit underprivileged children by buying them milk.

Castleberry had finished the season with a league scoring record, 126 points, while averaging 170 yards rushing per game. Numbers like that should have attracted a host of colleges, but there remained some doubt that Castleberry was big enough to play college ball. Georgia Tech, however, never wavered in its interest.

Coach Aleck recognized Castleberry's talents, even though they were housed in a diminutive package.

Castleberry had not yet made up his mind what school he would attend, but most knew that Georgia Tech had the inside track. Having grown up in Atlanta, Castleberry had always been a fan of Georgia Tech, and he liked the idea of remaining in Atlanta where he would be close to Shirley. Operating under her own belief that Clint would choose Georgia Tech, Shirley had already decided to attend Georgia State College for Women in Milledgeville, where she planned to study Spanish in advance of becoming a librarian. When asked why she'd chosen that school, she'd reply that her father's six sisters had all graduated there. But Shirley also knew that Georgia State College for Women allowed its students to go home for weekends, and she was looking forward to enjoying the college atmosphere at Georgia Tech on weekends with her beau. Shirley had done her homework. She knew that Wesleyan College in Macon, which she'd also considered, did not allow students to leave the campus on most weekends.

Tech won three games and lost six in 1941. Coach Aleck suddenly ranked as the oldest tenured head coach in the country after Illinois coach Bob Zuppke resigned following his twenty-ninth season. Since becoming head coach in 1920, Alexander had led his team to the Rose Bowl championship in the 1928 season and the Orange Bowl championship in the 1939 season—huge accomplishments in those years before the number of bowl games expanded dramatically. Otherwise, Coach Aleck's teams had been mediocre, but the cagey old coach understood his alumni base, and he understood the value of entertainment. Tech always played a heavyweight schedule, and the alumni loved the prospect of knocking off a big-time opponent almost as much as having a championship team.

The 1941 season was a case in point. Even though Tech had a losing season, they prospered at the gate. The Yellow Jackets drew 31,000 for a home game against Notre Dame and 32,000 for their finale against Georgia. For six home dates they drew 141,000, a highly respected figure for the day.

By December 7, Georgia Tech had completed its 1941 season save for an annual game with California that had been staged on a home-and-home basis since Tech's 8 – 7 win over California in the Rose Bowl game of January 1, 1929. Of the eight games that had been scheduled during the series, only six had been played. Tech's participation in the Orange Bowl caused one of the games to be canceled, and another had been canceled due to a California Rose Bowl bid. The Monday after Pearl Harbor, Alexander called his team together and asked them whether they should go to California as planned or call the game off.

"Being a junior, I was ready to go," said Bob Sheldon, a junior tailback on the team. "But the seniors were getting ready to graduate and go into the military, and they figured they ought to have as much time at home as they could. So they called off the game. We didn't go out there."

Among the additional concerns was finding adequate transportation to California. Tech had been told by the railroads that large parties would be difficult to accommodate. Then too, the Golden State appeared to be the most likely target of a Japanese attack against the United States mainland, and such an attack made sense given that much of America's military buildup for the coming war was taking place in California.

The attack on Pearl Harbor had left Americans angry and in shock, and those emotions were channeled into a unified support for the fight against Japan. Volunteers across the country continued to stand in line to enlist for military service. Protecting the American way of life, a way of life that had been threatened in such a heinous fashion, had become a national obsession. A common thread of patriotism ran from coast to coast, and the war effort took precedence over everything, relegating college football to a secondary pursuit. Just how much college football would be affected by the war remained to be seen.

Once the California game had been canceled, Coach Aleck and Bobby Dodd did what all coaches do at the conclusion of a season: they turned their attention toward the next year. Although the 1942 college football season might be canceled, going about their business as usual seemed the only practical approach. If the season did get canceled, there was nothing they could do about it, but if a season was played, they needed to be ready. When asked, Coach Aleck said that he did not know how the war would affect the 1942 season. "But I'll be looking around for a lot of youngsters to play," he said. "Looks like we all will have to use what we have."

Typical of Coach Aleck, he then offered a grin: "You won't catch me giving out scholarships to anybody over 19 years old."

Quite apart from the chaos and the great unknowns facing the next season, Coach Aleck and Bobby Dodd also found themselves at professional crossroads of a more personal sort. Coach Aleck wasn't getting any younger, and Dodd, though earmarked to become Coach Aleck's successor, had reached the point of needing to become a head coach before that ship left the harbor. A winning 1942 season could propel each of them in the direction he needed to head.

Assessing the talent on the Tech team, the pair knew they needed to find a fire starter, a special player who could give Georgia Tech an edge. Rumors were already circulating that if the 1942 season did take place, freshmen would be eligible to play. That made the idea of finding the player they needed among the ranks of high school seniors highly enticing; if the rumors proved true, such a recruit could play Tech football in 1942. And Coach Aleck and Dodd knew that such a rare talent lived and breathed less than five miles away from where Tech played each Saturday. Getting Castleberry into the Tech backfield looked like a recipe for returning to the top of the college football world, and signing him to a scholarship became a top priority.

* * * * *

Accolades and honors continued to flood in for Boys' High's 1941 season and for the players who had made the undefeated campaign so special. At a banquet at the historic Biltmore Hotel, Boys' High principal H.O. Smith declared the 1941 team the best in school history. Each player was awarded a miniature gold football for being part of a state championship team, while Castleberry and several of his teammates received additional gold footballs for making the All-G.I.A.A. team as chosen by the organization's coaches. A speaker from the Atlanta Kiwanis brought loud applause when he announced that Lee Edwards High would be bringing 2,000 fans from Asheville to the Milk Bowl. But the biggest thrill of the gala came at the end, when "motion pictures" were shown featuring the

Boys' High games with Tech High and Miami High along with footage from University of Georgia and University of Florida contests. Many in the audience concluded that Miami High had benefited greatly from several botched offsides calls during the Stingarees' touchdown drive that had tied the game at 7 – 7.

Doyal, who thought his team could beat any team in the country, had tried to settle some scores after the season by challenging Meridian High and Miami High to rematches. Both had declined. Shortly after Boys' High stopped "The Gray Streak in the Blue Grass" while dismantling Hopkinsville, Chicago's Roosevelt High also decided to cancel a date against the Purples.

Days before the game against Lee Edwards High, Castleberry and his Boys' High teammates learned about the fate of Kaye Thompkins, a fifth-grader from Atlanta's Mary Linn Elementary School. Thompkins had been stricken with infantile paralysis in late August, which forced him to spend a month in an iron lung, literally fighting for his life. Somehow the youngster had managed to survive. Thompkins's constant companions during his isolation were the voices on the radio and the words inside the sports section, which made Castleberry and Boys' High his favorites. Castleberry clearly held the status as the boy's hero. Understanding Thompkins's plight and the high esteem in which he held them, Castleberry and his teammates made a hospital visit, during which Thompkins seemed to glow in their presence. After the visit, Thompkins's mother introduced herself to Castleberry, telling him how her son talked of him ceaselessly and how following the team's season and his heroics had gone a long way toward keeping up her son's morale.

* * * * *

New Year's Day 1942 brought an interesting twist to college football.

Three weeks after Pearl Harbor, there was wide concern that Japan might find the large crowd gathered at the Rose Bowl an irresistible target. Accordingly, the U.S. Government ordered Earl Warren, the governor of California, to cancel the Rose Bowl game between Oregon State, winner of the Pacific Coast Conference, and its invited guest, Duke. (Tradition for the Rose Bowl dictated that the winner of the Pacific Coast Conference would pick its opponent.) Before the game was canceled, however, an idea took root to relocate it instead. Two alternate sites were proposed to the Tournament of Roses Association: Chicago's Soldier Field, which seated 120,000, and Durham, North Carolina, which promised to expand the seating capacity of Duke's home field from 35,000 to 55,000 by installing temporary stands. Ultimately, Durham was chosen to host the event.

Many of the players would be participating in their final game before going off to war, and both teams had already lost players to enlistment, while others had gone home after hearing reports that the game had been canceled. Duke's remaining players were unhappy with the new venue because they had looked forward to a true Rose Bowl experience before enlisting. Instead, they would be locked into practices at Durham and, to make matters worse, would miss what might be their last holiday at home before heading overseas. Duke finally granted its players time off prior to the game.

The Rose Bowl, which reigned as college football's premier event at the time, refunded approximately $64,000 in ticket revenues. Despite the difficulties and the endless scrambling, the 1942 Rose Bowl in Durham—the only time to this day the Rose Bowl has ever been played anywhere other than Pasadena—went on as planned in sloppy and wet conditions. Oregon State upset the previously undefeated Duke team 20 – 16.

Most of the players suiting up for the 1942 Rose Bowl would serve in the military before the end of War II. Four players from that game died in the war, including Al Hoover, who smothered a Japanese hand grenade to save several soldiers during the Battle of Peleliu Island.

Wallace Wade, who coached Duke in the Rose Bowl, experienced an odd coincidence during the Battle of the Bulge when he was served coffee and food by Stan Czech, who had played tackle for Oregon State against Duke. Eventually they realized their connection.

Duke's Charlie Haynes and Oregon State's Frank Parker served in the same battalion in Italy, where Parker helped save Haynes's life. When Haynes was wounded in the Arno River campaign, Parker was one of the men who carried him to safety.

On the day of the Rose Bowl, farther south in Atlanta, a football game of much greater local consequence was played. Over 22,000 fans packed the stands at Ponce de Leon Park for the Milk Bowl between Boys' High and Lee Edwards High. Castleberry's presence wasn't the only reason the New Year's Day game received so much attention. The team from Ashville featured a highly touted talent by the name of Charlie "Choo Choo" Justice, and the undefeated line of Lee Edwards High outweighed Boys' High's by an average of 25 pounds.

Lee Edwards High's contingent included 39 players—a large squad for the time—and needed three buses just to haul their band to the game. But Castleberry's music was the only sound heard on that rainy New Year's Day in Atlanta. Before most fans were seated, Castleberry returned a punt 46 yards to Lee Edwards's 24-yardline. On the next play, he hauled in a touchdown pass thrown by guard Leerie Jenkins, and the rout had begun.

Boys' High forced Lee Edwards to punt on its next possession, and Justice punted the ball into his blocker. The Purples recovered at the Lee Edwards 38. Castleberry got the ball on the first play on a reverse and slithered through the defense for another touchdown.

Castleberry's signature play of the game came early in the second quarter when Justice cut loose with a booming 50-yard punt. Castleberry fielded the punt at the Purples' 30, darted toward the right sideline, made a sharp cut in the opposite direction, and ran diagonally toward the other side of the field, splashing through mud and ankle-deep water all the way to the end zone. True to Doyal's nature, Castleberry sat out most of the remainder of the game, which Boys' High won 44 – 0 to complete the finest season in its history.

Justice went on to become a three-time All-America selection at the University of North Carolina, and years later he spoke about the New Year's Day contest in Atlanta.

"I was playing against Clint Castleberry and Boys' High in Atlanta in 1941 at old Ponce de Leon Park," Justice said. "We were undefeated, and it was supposed to be a big deal, me going against Clint Castleberry. Well, it was a big deal for Boys' High. Man, they wore us out."

Two days after the game, Castleberry and his teammates remembered their new friend and made a return visit to Thompkins, surrounding him in his bed so he could look over his toes at the foot of his bed and directly into Castleberry's eyes. They talked about the Milk Bowl and all the plays that had come alive in Thompkins's head while listening on the radio. Thompkins's hero had lived up to expectations during the football game, and he did so during the visit, handing the youngster the ball that had been used during Boys' High's win over Tech High.

· · · · ·

On February 23, 1942, a Japanese submarine surfaced a half-mile off the coast of Ellwood, California, and began shelling the oil refinery 12 miles west of Santa Barbara. While the physical damage caused by Japan's first attack on the U.S. mainland was minimal, the psychological damage was immense, validating the fears of many that Japan could successfully attack the West Coast. In the aftermath, on March 2, the U.S. government began the internment of Japanese-American citizens.

At the time, of course, it was assumed that Japan had launched the attack for propaganda purposes and to probe America's defenses, but a different explanation emerged years later in a 1982 issue of *Parade* magazine. According to that article, the Japanese submarine commander Nishino Kozo had been the skipper of an oil tanker that had regularly visited that particular refinery prior to the war. During one visit in the late 1930s, Kozo had made his way up a path from the beach to a grand ceremony saluting him and his crew. Inexplicably, he had slipped and fallen, landing on a prickly-pear cactus, which necessitated having cactus needles removed from his buttocks. Laughter from workers on an oil rig accompanied the episode, further humiliating the commander and prompting him to swear he would claim revenge. If this explanation is correct, the attack was of a personal nature and not a strategic assault by the Japanese navy.

In March 1942, Castleberry made his decision to attend Georgia Tech. Tech had always been at the top of his list, and the idea of playing for the Yellow Jackets finally won out. He accepted the football scholarship offered him by Coach Aleck.

Castleberry's signing came shortly after the announcement that Tech had hired Shorty Doyal's assistant, Dwight Keith, to become the freshman and B team coach. Keith had been Boys' High's head

Dwight Keith coached Clint Castleberry at Boys' High and followed him to Georgia Tech.

basketball coach and the backfield coach for the football team; he also published a sports magazine. Castleberry and Keith had a good relationship, and many who knew Castleberry figured that Coach Aleck had hedged his bets by bringing Keith aboard.

Castleberry had another compelling reason for choosing Tech, however, as his brother Jimmy later clarified. "He was either going to Georgia or Georgia Tech," said Jimmy in a 1989 interview with *The Atlanta Constitution*. "He elected to go with Coach Aleck, and the major reason was that he was in love and wanted to stay in Atlanta."

Shirley Poole was happy with her boyfriend's decision, but she said she had not wielded her influence to get him to remain in Atlanta. "That was his decision," she said.

Understandably, Georgia Tech and the University of Georgia both scrambled to bring Boys' High players into the fold. Few high school football players in the Southeast could claim a higher pedigree than to have played for Shorty Doyal. Raymond Smith and Bill Magbee joined Castleberry at Tech, while Charlie Furchgott,

Joe Kennimer, Jimmy Gordon, and Myrtus Maffett all went to Georgia.

A week after signing with Tech, Castleberry played his final football game at Boys' High, leading a 31 – 0 romp by the alumni team over the Boys' High team that would defend the Purples' state title in the fall of 1942. Castleberry scored twice in the contest, and for one of the few times while playing football at Boys' High, he got to play an entire game.

* * * * *

In the pantheon of Boys' High royalty, Castleberry was king.

On May 29, 1942, Bing Crosby recorded Irving Berlin's "White Christmas" in 18 minutes for the movie *Holiday Inn*; the song would become the biggest-selling record in history. That same day, a hundred Boys' High athletes were honored during a gathering at the Druid Hills Baptist Church for giving the school its most successful sports year in the history of the school. Castleberry, who had already been acclaimed many times over as the greatest athlete in the school's history, was awarded a pen and pencil set by the school's alumni, who voted him the most representative Boys' High athlete. The modest gift was characteristic of an era that eschewed pretentious trophies for the smallest of accomplishments. Castleberry's teammates showed their love and appreciation for Castleberry with a roaring ovation. Typical of Castleberry, he blushed at the recognition.

Doyal called Castleberry "the best all-around athlete we ever had at Boys' High," and for good reason. He never played in a losing football game for the Purples, and, in addition to making all-state in football, he did the same in basketball and baseball.

"He was such a great hitter and center fielder. I think that actually was his best sport," Doyal said. "He was a great competitor."

7

Will There be a Season?

In 1942, Georgia Tech found itself deeply immersed in the war effort. The school's curriculum emphasized aeronautics, physics, chemistry, and mechanical and electrical engineering. Who better than the professors who taught those subjects to help conduct research for the war effort and offer technical training all over the United States? Georgia Tech professors were in great demand, and a horde of new students—freshmen through seniors—arrived on campus to fill new programs supporting military needs. ROTC assumed a higher profile, as instruction in the tactics of war acquired a new sense of urgency. Students were even taught gunnery on Rose Bowl Field, where the Tech football team practiced. Army Specialized Training Programs, designed to train "high-grade technicians and specialists," also came to the campus.

Amid these realigned priorities, college football teetered on shaky footing. Gridiron heroes from all over the country were wearing combat helmets instead of the leather models fashioned for Saturday-afternoon warriors. The countless coaches and players serving their country's military threw the wisdom of continuing college football into question. Many felt that the sport should be discontinued while the nation was at war.

Campus leaders at Georgia Tech and Georgia were among those suggesting that football be canceled in 1942. Georgia Governor Eugene Talmadge wrapped himself in the flag, noting, "We're doing everything for winning the war, if it takes putting our debutantes to hoeing potatoes." But Talmadge remained on the fence when it came to canceling football in the South.

The arguments against conducting a football season included travel restrictions in addition to the loss of coaches and players to military service. With gasoline, rubber, and train and bus use all redirected to military purposes, just getting teams and fans to distant games would be difficult. (The need for rationing was clear. For example, America's 29 million passenger cars used 75% of the nation's rubber for tires immediately prior to the war, but the Japanese capture of Malaya and the Dutch East Indies almost eliminated the import of plantation rubber. The development of synthetic rubber became a top priority, and in the meantime, the available supply of natural rubber went to the war effort.) Games under the lights were forbidden in coastal cities.

But the morale of the country—as well as the morale of those in the military—argued strongly for keeping college football rolling. In addition, there was a good argument that college physical education programs in general and college football in particular could help build strong soldiers and leaders. And last but not least, war bonds could be promoted through college football. The bonds, which helped finance the war, sold for 75 percent of face value and yielded a 2.9 percent return after a ten-year maturity.

Once the decision was made to play the season, the problem of finding players to fill college rosters loomed. Men between the ages of 20 and 44 were eligible for the draft. College freshmen had been allowed to play during World War I, but they had become ineligible again after the war.

More than 200 players from the Southeastern Conference, plus 25 coaches, assistant coaches, and trainers, went off to military service between January 1 and August 1, 1942. Acknowledging the problem, the Southeastern Conference, along with other conferences in the country, began to give serious consideration to the idea of allowing freshmen to play varsity sports.

Finding coaches—particularly assistants—also proved difficult due to the enlistments. Many programs promoted assistant coaches into vacant head-coach jobs, thereby creating vacancies among assistants. The University of Oregon went through three head coaches in three days. If ever a buyer's market for college football coaches existed, this was it. The following appeared in *The Saturday Evening Post:* "One veteran [coach] owes his job to the Japs. A meeting which had been called to give him the bounce was called off when war was declared, and now the old-timer is reported coming up with his best squad in years."

Georgia Tech was given little hope for a strong 1942 season based on the previous season's 3 – 6 mark and a schedule that included Notre Dame, Navy, Alabama, Auburn, and Georgia, all of which were highly ranked nationally. The experts had Tech finishing as low as eighth in the 12-team SEC. Football experts also felt, however, that the season could turn into a wild scramble in which traditional heavyweights might be overthrown and the rankings scrambled by the impact of military enlistments.

Wrote Francis Wallace of *The Saturday Evening Post,* "Precisely because of its imperfections, football is likely to be more exciting, more colorful than ever."

Between the end of the 1941 college football season and the beginning of the 1942 season, the issue of freshman eligibility rose and fell like a stock market index. Schools and conferences debated the issues at conference and faculty meetings without consensus. In January 1942, however, Harvard announced that it would make freshmen eligible for varsity competition during the war and would also condense its academic program from four years to three by eliminating the summer break, thereby preparing students more quickly for the officer corps or wartime industries.

The Missouri Valley Conference likewise approved freshman eligibility, while the Southern and Southeastern conferences continued to weigh their options. The Big Ten and Pacific Coast conferences decided against freshman participation in intercollegiate athletics, while in February, Yale joined its rivals Harvard and Princeton in declaring freshmen eligible.

Such decisions paled in significance to those being made in conjunction with the war effort. On January 19, 1942, President Roosevelt went to Congress to ask for an appropriation of $28.5

billion for the war effort, increasing the overall war budget to $103.5 billion, a staggering sum at the time.

Following war news quickly became a national obsession, and the news wasn't good in early 1942. On February 15, the Japanese took Singapore after a two-week siege, giving them control of a critical portion of the sea route connecting Europe and Asia. Some 130,000 Allied troops were captured in the surrender, the largest in British military history.

Even more devastating news came in March, when the nation learned that General Douglas MacArthur had abandoned the Philippines and escaped to Australia in the face of a withering Japanese assault. MacArthur's Far East Air Force had been destroyed on the ground by a surprise Japanese attack on December 8, the day after Pearl Harbor, and Japanese forces landed on Luzon later in December. MacArthur's American and Filipino troops were defending the Bataan peninsula and Corregidor Island, in Manila Bay—where MacArthur had his headquarters—when Roosevelt ordered MacArthur to escape to Australia. Upon arriving in Australia on March 20, MacArthur made his famous proclamation to the Filipino people, "I shall return."

The bad news continued when Japanese forces captured 36,000 American and Filipino prisoners at Bataan on April 9 after a three-month siege and six-day pitched battle. Surviving prisoners of war were then forced on the infamous 60-mile Bataan Death March, though the American public would not learn of this until January 1944.

Hearing such news fueled fear in a country accustomed to freedom. The possibility of losing that freedom to the iron rule of a barbaric enemy put the military effort above all else.

Good news, on the other hand, had another effect—inspiring able-bodied men of fighting age to take part in defending the country—and April 18, 1942 brought just such good news. Reports reached home that American B-25 bombers led by General James Doolittle had bombed Tokyo after taking off from the aircraft carrier *Hornet* some 600 miles from the coast of Japan. For months the Japanese war machine had been battering the Allies in the Pacific, but now America was hitting back.

Unknown to the United States and the rest of the world at the time, the Germans sent 1,500 Jews to the gas chambers at

Auschwitz on May 12, 1942. And horrific though it was, that geno-
cide paled in comparison to the aggregate number of deaths at the
camp. Rudolph Hess would testify at the Nuremberg Tribunal on
April 15, 1946, that from May 1940 through December 1943, the
time during which the camp was under his command, at least 2.5
million men, women, and children died at the camp by poison gas
and incineration, while another half million died from starvation
and disease.

The war crept closer to home on May 12, 1942, when a German U-boat torpedoed a cargo ship at the mouth of the Mississippi River, sinking the vessel and killing 27 crew members. By
mid-May, the threat of attack from German or Japanese sub-
marines had become all too real. Some 159 ships had been sunk
since America's entry into the war by enemy subs off U.S. coasts,
leaving 999 dead and 1,212 missing. (Another 4,900 crew members had survived the attacks.) Cargo vessels were in constant danger of being torpedoed in the shipping lanes, and troops traveling
to the front lines overseas were repeatedly lost at sea before reaching their destinations. Because ships steaming at night were more
visible targets when silhouetted against well-lit shorelines, blackout policies were instituted, restricting nighttime lighting in towns
and cities with populations of more than 5,000 within 30 miles of
the coast.

In the South these lighting constraints included parts of North
Carolina, South Carolina, and Georgia and all of Florida. The sense
of vulnerability to enemy attack intensified with this policy, one
more factor prompting able-bodied men—and particularly young
men—to want to enlist in order to help preserve the American way.
Clint Castleberry was no different.

"Clint wanted to fight," Shirley Poole said. "All of the boys did.
Things were a lot different back then."

Castleberry enrolled at Georgia Tech in June 1942 and enlisted
in the Army Air Corps Reserves on July 2, though it was reported
at the time that he would finish his studies at Georgia Tech before
becoming subject to duty. "Most of the team did sign up, and almost
90 percent of them were gone [off to war] after the '42 season," said
Joe Daniel, a freshman defensive end and teammate of Castleberry
in 1942.

Castleberry's family had no qualms about his signing up for military service.

"When he joined, there was no question about it," Jimmy Castleberry said. "There was no discussion. That was just the thing you did. Everybody was anxious to get in. It was a given. You'd have to have lived in that time to know that the only thought was beating those Germans."

Though the war took top billing, the fall football season was on the immediate horizon. By August, Coach Aleck was allowing himself to believe that freshmen would be allowed to play in the SEC. An earlier vote of conference representatives had been deadlocked at 6 – 6 on the question, but two of the schools voting no had since become vocal about having changed their minds. The conference had scheduled a revote in Atlanta on September 18—just before the start of the season—and most considered the outcome a foregone conclusion. By the time fall football practice began at Georgia Tech, Coach Aleck and other coaches in the conference were inclined to prepare as if any freshman player on the squad would be eligible.

8

A Freshman Opens Eyes

Following his established fall tradition, Coach Aleck posted an announcement of the first day of football practice—which was September 1 in 1942—a week prior to the day. The notice normally enticed 80 to 90 players to attend that first practice, and the coach and his staff would pare that number down to 35 or so.

Like other college coaches at the time, Coach Aleck faced personnel problems due to the war. He had hoped, for example, to have Gene Leonard anchoring his 1942 line. A high school heavyweight wrestling champion, Leonard was one of the best line prospects Coach Aleck had ever had. Instead, Leonard chose to leave for the battlefield when an opportunity presented itself. His departure left a void at guard and tackle.

Tech also had vacancies in its coaching ranks to fill. Mack Tharpe, Tech's long-time line coach, had enlisted in the navy in the spring. A Tech graduate who had played football for Coach Aleck in the 1920s, Tharpe had been working at a local insurance agency and coaching college football during fall afternoons. Unknown to most, he had begun sneaking off to take flying lessons several years prior to the outbreak of World War II. He entered the navy at age 38, hoping to become a fighter pilot while understanding that his age would probably prevent him from fulfilling that dream. Coach Aleck was one of the few people who had known of Tharpe's flying lessons, and as Tharpe's mentor and friend, had advised him to enter the navy as a physical instructor and then "start trying" to cajole his way into the opportunity he so wanted. If Tharpe were a good enough flyer and military man, the navy might eventually see things his way.

Now Coach Aleck needed a replacement for Tharpe, and he found a candidate in his own backyard. Bob Miller, a Tech chemical engineering professor who had played center for Ohio State in the early 1930s, volunteered for the job. Coach Aleck listened carefully to Miller's pitch and left their meeting convinced he could do the job. Miller joined the staff while continuing his teaching duties.

Of the 91 players who suited up for Tech's first two-hour practice, 35 were selected for the varsity squad. They included three freshmen: Castleberry, Bill Healy, and Raymond Smith, who was a Boys' High teammate of Clint. After a summer in which prospective players had been allowed to conduct informal training sessions, the team showed up in its best physical condition in years.

From the outset, the Yellow Jackets' single-wing backfield appeared set in stone—or at least, that was the appearance Coach Aleck sought to give. Wilber Stein and Jack Faulkner were to split duties at blocking back; Ralph Plaster and Bobby Dodd (no relation to the coach) were scheduled to do the same at fullback; Pat McHugh and Jim Luck had the wingback duties; and Bobby Sheldon, Eddie Prokop, and Davey Eldredge were lined up to play tailback—a position that called for both running and passing skills. Keeping Castleberry under wraps fit perfectly the way Coach Aleck liked to go about his business.

Platoon football, position specialization, and endless substitutions were not yet a part of college football in 1942. A football player needed to possess both offensive and defensive skills.

Tech practices took place at Rose Bowl Field, named accordingly because funds from Tech's appearance in the 1929 Rose Bowl had been used to buy the land for the team practice field. These practices weren't cut from typical cloth. In the 1940s, most head coaches were despots. They reigned supreme. Nobody questioned a coach's authority or anything he did. A yes-sir, no-sir, no-nonsense mentality was expected, and on the field, toughness ruled. Practices were about being tough—suck it up, go harder—the drill sergeant approach. Fun had no place in the game. But none of this was true at Tech except that players were expected to be respectful of their coaches.

"Coach Aleck and Bobby Dodd remembered that football was a game," Joe Daniel said. "So they tried to make a game out of it. Practice was a game. I think in some ways, that's why they were able to get more out of their boys than some coaches. I can't even begin to tell you what nice guys Coach Aleck and Bobby Dodd were. They made football fun."

Tech players were under no compunction to prove their toughness with macho displays in order to win a spot on the team. Instead, Coach Aleck relied on scrimmages to tell him who should be on the field for the Yellow Jackets. Nor did he believe in separate dormitories for the athletes. He wanted them to have the same experience as other college students, living and eating with them as well as joining fraternities. The football team did not have special meal tables; team members ate their meals in Brittain Hall, the primary dining facility on the east side of the campus.

True to Coach Aleck's wishes, Castleberry joined the Phi Delta Theta fraternity. He lived on the second floor of Cloudman Dorm, which ran adjacent to Grant Field on the opposite side of Techwood Drive. He could literally walk across the street to dress at Grant Field for practice. Beginning in the fall quarter, Don Paschal joined Castleberry as his roommate. The pair had attended kindergarten, grammar school, junior high, and high school together, always best friends. They had gone their separate ways when Paschal had accepted a football scholarship to South Carolina, but after spending the summer at South Carolina, Paschal decided to transfer to Tech, where he played on the freshman team in 1942. Among the other members of Georgia Tech's 1942 freshman class was a skinny young man from Plains, Georgia, named Jimmy Carter, who would become the thirty-ninth president of the United States.

Tech's locker-room facility comprised a series of rooms cuddled underneath the stands backing the north end zone of Grant Field.

Within those confines were lockers, showers, and plenty of tables for rubdowns. Weight rooms did not yet exist. On practice days, many players arrived unsure whether they would find a blue varsity jersey hanging in their locker or a red one to assign them to the scout team that day. Once dressed, the teammates made their way a half-mile across campus to Rose Bowl Field for practice.

Downtown Atlanta stood within walking distance of the Tech campus, further enhancing the experience of being a Georgia Tech student. Atlanta had a vibrant and progressive feeling in 1942. Approximately one-third of the city's population of close to 500,000 was black. Coca Cola maintained a huge local presence, Delta Airlines had moved its headquarters to Atlanta, and the town of Marietta, just outside the Atlanta city limits, became the home of the Bell assembly plant of B-29 bombers, creating 40,000 local jobs.

Castleberry immediately began to distinguish himself in Tech practices, validating everything Coach Aleck and Dodd had believed about the Boys' High talent they had coveted. "When I was a freshman, we scrimmaged against the varsity a lot," Joe Daniel said. "There weren't a lot of boys out for ball, and the varsity played both ways—that's the way football was in those days. So our scrimmages were just played like that. Head on. Since we didn't have many players, everybody got a shot at showing what they could do. Castleberry stuck out like you wouldn't believe. Talk about being elusive. Trying to tackle him was like trying to catch a butterfly. He was fantastic. You'd have a head-on shot against him, and he was so quick that he just wouldn't be there."

Defensive end John Crawford was among the upperclassmen to marvel at Castleberry's talents.

"I was amazed the way he could handle a football," Crawford said. "Especially running. He threw left-handed, which seemed to be an advantage because that could be tricky for a defense. He could do it all, especially punt returning."

Though the Southeastern Conference had not yet approved the use of freshmen, Crawford could see that Coach Aleck was counting heavily on having the freshman for the season. In essence, Castleberry would be his secret weapon. Since Coach Aleck considered Castleberry a valuable asset, he looked out for his welfare, which extended away from the football field.

Alexander had always roamed the Tech campus freely and knew the pulse of any activity that went on. Now he happened to come upon Castleberry participating in a pick-up basketball game. Castleberry loved basketball and planned on playing for the Tech team once football season had run its course.

"Clint was a good basketball player, and he was scrimmaging with us, and Coach Aleck was on the side lines," said George William Rogers, a classmate of Castleberry at Tech. "He saw Clint get bumped around rebounding and called him over. He said, 'You can't play this sport. You don't have all the pads on.' He wouldn't let him play. I remember that distinctly."

Coach Aleck's caution was understandable given the impact Castleberry made on the team as early as his first practice. He ran for a touchdown the first time he touched the ball, leaving the team's upperclassmen stunned at what they witnessed.

Years later Dodd wrote about Castleberry for a *Saturday Evening Post* series by coaches entitled "The Best Player I Ever Coached." *Atlanta Journal* sports columnist Furman Bisher served as the ghostwriter for Dodd's piece:

"It was 1942—the first war year freshmen were eligible for varsity play—that Clint came to us straight out of Boys' High School in Atlanta. As Bill Alexander's backfield coach, I welcomed him— and gave him an awful job for an eighteen-year-old. In our single-wing offense, Clint was called on both at tailback and wingback. He quickly showed vast speed, quick reaction, fine personality and terrific competitive spirit—all the physical assets of a truly great back, in fact, except one: He lacked size. At most, he stood a bow-legged five feet nine and weighed 155 pounds. But he never let that stop him."

Coach Aleck favored the single-wing offense because he never felt that Tech had enough manpower to employ a T-formation. Castleberry's talents were perfect for a single-wing, since cutbacks were especially effective from the formation, which would see the tailback run to the strong side with a pulling guard and the quarterback (often called the blocking back) leading the blocking. The defensive end usually determined whether or not the play would be successful, since it was his responsibility to prevent the ball carrier from getting to the outside. If he couldn't protect the outside, the back would turn the corner and cut upfield—but if he cheated too far outside to prevent that, one of the lead blockers could simply seal him off out there, allowing the tailback to cut inside—or "cut back"—and take the ball up the field.

Two simple plays prevented defenses from stacking up against the cutback play. In one, the tailback would pretend to take the snap from center when in fact the ball would go to the fullback, who would run into the middle of the line. Dodd's version of this included an added element of deception. The fullback and tailback would position themselves so close together (in what was known as the "30 series") that defenses had an especially difficult time sorting out which of them had received the snap.

The other play to keep defenses honest was a wingback reverse, which punished any defenders who overpursued while trying to stop the cutback play. Dodd's version had the ball snapped to the fullback, who would do a half turn and hand it off to the halfback or wingback on the reverse. Dodd's wrinkles brought a deceptive element to the offense.

Tech entered the season with good passers in Eddie Prokop and Bobby Sheldon, and they were counting on Castleberry's accurate left-handed arm as well. Castleberry's talents were perfectly suited to the tailback and wingback positions in the single-wing offense.

Having upperclassmen accept a freshman into the starting ranks might have been a tricky proposition had that freshman been anyone but Castleberry. He had two major pluses going for him in winning over his older teammates. First, he did not have an inflated ego, so his personality didn't rub upperclassmen players the wrong way. Second, his talent was obvious, and athletes recognize and respect talent. Playing against the swivel-hipped freshman, the upperclassmen could clearly see that he possessed special skills. Castleberry's standing with the upperclassmen never became an issue.

Sheldon remembered the first time he met Castleberry, who was trying to get a handle on the nuances of the single-wing.

"He came up to me at practice and asked me if I would help him learn the Georgia Tech system before practice, you know, get out to practice early," Sheldon said. "Because Boys' High always ran the Notre Dame system, the Box. And I was delighted to do it. I think that showed Clint's character. He was heralded by a lot of colleges, but he came to Tech and did not act like he thought he was a star. Everybody liked him right away. He was just that type of guy. He was almost too good to be true."

Two days before the final vote on freshman eligibility by the Southeastern Conference, Castleberry made jaws drop at practice when he fielded a punt during a scrimmage and zigzagged his way through defenders en route to a touchdown. On another play out of the single-wing, two defenders converged on him only to end up in each other's arms in an almost cartoonish pose, wondering in disbelief how the freshman sensation had squirted through their grasp so quickly. Castleberry scored on the play. If his teammates hadn't already been convinced what kind of season the team might have with him in the lineup, that practice erased any doubts.

Castleberry's offensive exploits gathered most of the praise, but he brought the same athleticism to the other side of the ball. A sure-handed tackler with extraordinary pass-coverage skills, he was an impact player as a defensive back as well. An unnamed Tech assistant told the *The Atlanta Constitution* that Castleberry was "one of those football naturals who come along not oftener than once in a decade."

The Atlanta Journal wrote of Castleberry, "The lad has poise and skill beyond most . . . [freshmen] their first year out of high school."

In keeping with his understated approach, Coach Aleck continued to downplay the impact Castleberry might have on the team's fortunes if freshmen were made eligible. Deception was not just a key to Alexander's offense, it was central to his coaching philosophy, right down to the sedate, mustard-colored jerseys and plain pants the team wore. Tech players looked undersized and slow wearing the uniforms, and Coach Aleck liked it that way.

Castleberry had not yet played even a down of college football and might not have done so for another year if the voting on freshman eligibility at the Southeastern Conference meeting had for any reason gone differently than expected. Southeastern Conference officials met as scheduled in Atlanta on September 18, 1942, to decide the freshman eligibility issue once and for all. Prior to the vote, Tulane's athletic director Wilbur Smith argued against allowing freshmen to play. Since the prospects of having a college football season in 1943 were dim anyway, he reasoned, it made no sense to alter the rules for the 1942 season.

"Why can't we do the best we can with what we've got?" Smith asked. "I don't think it [the use of freshmen] will help the conferences at all."

James D. Hoskins, president of the University of Tennessee, argued the case for freshman eligibility, noting, "If we're going to have football, let's have the finest we can."

Conference presidents met first, mulling five different proposals regarding freshmen and transfer students. An executive session then took place behind closed doors, and when the doors reopened, the 12-member organization announced a vote of 9 – 3 in favor of allowing freshmen to be eligible for the duration of the war. Auburn, Florida, Georgia, Georgia Tech, Louisiana State, Mississippi, Mississippi State, Tennessee, and Vanderbilt had all voted for the plan; Alabama, Kentucky, and Tulane had voted against it.

Georgia Tech had further proposed that all restrictions be waived for junior college transfers and for transfers from colleges that had abandoned athletics, but the group voted down the Tech proposal.

There remained a gray area regarding the status of freshmen when SEC teams played teams from conferences that did not allow freshmen to be eligible. SEC schools had contests scheduled against teams from the Southern, Southwestern, and Pacific Coast conferences, none of which allowed freshmen to play. On those occasions, it was decided, freshmen could play only if the opponent agreed.

Tech spirits were visibly lifted when news of the vote reached the practice on Rose Bowl field that afternoon. Clint Castleberry would be in the backfield when Tech opened the season on September 26 against Auburn at Grant Field.

9

A Monster in Athens

pproximately 70 miles northeast of Atlanta and Georgia Tech lies Athens, Georgia, home of the University of Georgia. Whenever the two schools competed in anything, hair rose on the backs of necks and blood began to boil. The rivalry came to be known as "Clean, Old-Fashioned Hate."

The earliest recorded animosity between the two schools dated back to 1891, when Georgia's school colors were anointed as crimson, black, and old gold. The color scheme was fine with one exception, according to the school's first football coach, Dr. Charles H. Herty, who felt that old gold suggested cowardice due to its resemblance to yellow. As it happened, Georgia Tech students selected old gold and white for their school colors that same year, and the Tech football team wore gold uniforms for their first game of 1891. Georgia fans saw this as Tech's way of thumbing their noses at the Bulldogs, and after the 1893 football game between the two schools, Herty had old gold removed from the Georgia color wheel.

Further animosity followed during World War I. Georgia ceased playing football from 1917 – 18 because most of the school's male students who were fit for military service had gone to war.

Tech continued its football program, however, because the military used Tech as a training ground, which left the school well supplied with young men for a team. Once Georgia resumed playing football in 1919, Georgia students directed relentless barbs toward Tech for having continued to play during the war.

The final straw came in the form of two floats in a Georgia parade in 1919. One float had been constructed to resemble a tank and had been inscribed, "UGA in Argonne." Argonne, of course, referred to the Argonne Forest, the site of some of World War I's heaviest fighting. Next in line behind the tank float came one resembling a yellow donkey, the sign on which read, "Tech in Atlanta."

After the parade, Tech and Georgia quit competing against each other for several years, and Tech refused to allow Georgia to use Grant Field as a result of the severed ties. Not until 1925 did the two schools agree to renew their athletic rivalry.

Coach Aleck and Wally Butts, who had coached the Bulldog football team since 1938, were about as different in their personalities and coaching philosophies as two coaches could be. Coach Aleck, though cranky at times, had a refined, educated manner and carried himself as a gentleman. Butts—who was nicknamed "the little round man" due to his squat, stout, five-foot, six-inch frame— could be nasty and mean and would never be mistaken for being refined. Coach Aleck preached defense and controlling the game, while Butts believed in the passing game, which made him something of an innovator in a time when most coaches favored the "three yards and a cloud of dust" approach. The two men shared little love.

"I thought [Butts] was an extremely good coach," said Charley Trippi, one of the primary cogs in the 1942 Georgia backfield. "One of the things that carried him to being a good coach was that he had extreme, hard discipline. He didn't tolerate anything from his ballplayers like what happens today. Even if you smoked back then, he'd chase you home, put you on a bus and say, 'Go on, you don't want to play football.' He was tough. And we performed under his guidance."

Georgia's prospects for the 1942 season were grand. They had finished the 1941 season with an 8 – 1 – 1 record and were ranked

Frankie Sinkwich running the football for the University of Geor-gia. The Bulldogs standout would win the 1942 Heisman Trophy.

fourteenth in the Associated Press preseason poll. In addition, the Bulldogs had Frankie Sinkwich in their backfield.

Sinkwich had grown up in Youngstown, Ohio, a tough Steel Belt city known as a breeding ground for football talent. Coincidence had brought him to Georgia when Butts's assistant Bill Hartman had made a trip to Ohio to recruit a running back said to be the best in the state.

By the time Hartman arrived, the prospect had already signed with Ohio State. Disgruntled, Hartman pulled his Plymouth into a local gas station to fill up before heading back to Athens, and it was then that a casual conversation with the pump attendant led to a complete change of fortune for the trip. Learning of Hartman's mission, the attendant told Hartman that a great ball player named Frankie Sinkwich had attended Chaney High School and lived near the station. Taking a chance, Hartman went to talk to Sinkwich, who became a Bulldog after Georgia agreed to offer a scholarship to his friend and high school teammate George Poschner, who had already graduated from high school and was working at a meat and produce market in Youngstown.

Poschner had already beaten the odds just by playing high school football. He had spent his first three years of high school as a cheerleader and band member, unable to make the football team in large part due to his size. He had weighed just 110 pounds as a freshman, but by the start of his senior year, he had grown considerably. Finally making the team, Poschner quickly became Sinkwich's favorite target.

Freshmen could not play varsity sports during Sinkwich's first year in Athens in 1939, so he was relegated to the freshman team. He became the cornerstone of that freshman squad, which came to be known as the "Point-a-Minute Bullpups," putting up point totals that would shame a basketball team. That team now comprised the nucleus of Georgia's 1942 varsity squad.

Sinkwich played hard-nosed football and had obvious talent, and other players respected him. After he led Georgia to a 21 – 19 win over Tech in 1941, Tech players called him "the best" and "the cleanest" player they had played against, according to Tech trainer Claude Bond.

"I wish you'd put that in the paper because I think it is the truth," Bond told the press. "Our boys said that guy's interested in only one thing—getting that extra yard.'"

Sinkwich had evolved into a complete offensive leader, but his game started with his running. He led the nation in rushing yards in 1941, with 209 carries for 1,103 yards, which set up his passing. The Bulldogs had crushed Texas Christian in the Orange Bowl before a crowd of 35,786 in Miami on January 1, 1942.

Based on the Bulldogs' previous year's success and the addition to their team of Trippi—who had been a standout on the freshman team in 1941—their expectations for 1942 were off the charts. Even Butts tried to downplay the coming season. At an Atlanta Exchange Club luncheon in late August, the Georgia coach told the audience, "Our team plays eight of its eleven games away from home, and seven of them are with Southeastern Conference opponents. I think this conference is the fastest in America. We have more first-class teams here every year than any other section. It's tough to win 'em in this league."

Georgia's odd schedule stemmed from the fact that Athens

was not a large population center. Had the war—and gas rationing—not been an issue, Georgia fans from all over could easily have hopped into their cars and made the trek to Athens for the games. But the war changed that. Most citizens needed to preserve their meager gas allotments to get to work or for other necessary travel. Attending a football game was a luxury that could be foregone. Thus, a university like Georgia had to consider the gate for its games, and in many cases playing games away from Athens made more financial sense for the Bulldogs' athletic program. Georgia drew the line at playing their games against Tech and Tulane in Atlanta, however; the citizens of Athens wanted the games at home, and so did Georgia's student body, most of whom would have been unable to get to games in Atlanta due to transportation problems.

The Saturday Evening Post further fueled the early-season hype when, in his annual Pigskin Preview, Francis Wallace named Sinkwich his back of the year and tagged Georgia as the South's best team, picking the Bulldogs to meet Southern California in the Rose Bowl on New Year's Day. Such forecasts made the typical pessimistic, aw-shucks coach-speak difficult for Butts to pull off. Georgia had a monster team in 1942, and everybody knew it.

Butts was disappointed not to have more backups on his squad, but he understood the explosive possibilities of his starting personnel. The prospect of adding Trippi to the backfield with Sinkwich could no doubt brighten even his worst day, given how well the pair fit Georgia's single-wing attack.

"Frank was an extremely tough runner from tackle to tackle," Trippi said. "I liked the outside lanes more than he did. He sort of complemented me because he kept the interior linemen honest because of his ability to break tackles up the middle. Of course it opened up the outside lanes for me. So he was a tremendous complement to my game, really."

Not only was there plenty of room for both Trippi and Sinkwich on the field, they had no problems co-existing in the team leadership hierarchy either. Egos were not a problem.

"Sinkwich was a low-keyed sort of individual," Trippi said. "He didn't have much to say, but he played hard. That's all I can remember about him. I roomed next door to him. We didn't communicate too much; he was a low-key individual."

No player in the South carried a bigger aura than Sinkwich, and Castleberry could be counted among the legions who admired the Bulldog star. He mentioned on several occasions how much he thought of Sinkwich. Indeed, Castleberry considered Sinkwich the best football player in the country.

Entering the season, Georgia's players, like Tech's, faced the prospect of military service, and they knew what awaited them after the season.

"We had to sign up in the reserves to play football in '42,"Trippi said. "So as soon as the season was over, we were called. In April I got a uniform for the air force. It was predetermined what was going to transpire right after the football season."

Seizing the day to make the most of a college football experience had never meant more.

Butts rolled out his powerhouse 1942 squad in Louisville, where the Bulldogs opened the SEC schedule at the University of Kentucky's Manual Stadium. Butts and Kentucky coach Ab Kirwan were bitter adversaries dating back to their high school days, leading most to believe that the bad blood between the two coaches would spill over into the contest.

Leo Yarutis, a freshman guard from Gary, Indiana, took the field for Kentucky, thereby earning the distinction as the first freshman to play in an SEC game since World War I. Yarutis made an early impact in the game when Sinkwich went off tackle and Yarutis threw everybody's All-American for a one-yard loss. It was one of many great plays in the Wildcats' upset bid, but Sinkwich came up big when the Bulldogs needed him most. Holding a 7 – 6 lead with just over three minutes to go, the Bulldogs faced a fourth-and-two at their own 35 and lined up to punt. Sinkwich lined up as the punter, but after receiving the snap, he made a sharp cut to his left and picked up the first down. Georgia then kept the ball for the remainder of the game to avoid an upset.

Butts had little time to celebrate, since the team representing the Jacksonville Naval Air Base would be the Bulldogs' next opponent. Signaling the unpredictability of every college roster in the country, this would-be cupcake on the Georgia schedule appeared to have teeth after beating the University of Florida 20 – 7.

10

A Freshmen Sensation Arrives

Sixty U.S. colleges opted to shut down their football programs prior to the start of the 1942 season. Transportation would be a problem all season due to such wartime restrictions as the unavailability of chartered buses, which prompted many games to be shifted from small college towns to larger cities with their larger fan bases. The Illinois – Ohio State game was moved from Champaign to Cleveland, and Stanford's games with Santa Clara and Washington were moved from Palo Alto to San Francisco. Texas A&M moved its game with Rice from College Station to Houston.

Addressing the Atlanta Touchdown Club during a weekday luncheon prior to Tech's opening contest against Auburn, Coach Aleck stated his belief that college football would again have a season in 1943, despite the war effort. Though most colleges had instituted speed-up curricula that would allow students to graduate in three years rather than four so they could be funneled into the armed forces, Coach Aleck reasoned that the military still needed an officer corps of men educated in engineering and mathematics. In addition, those young men left behind—as well as those too young or too old to fight—needed a diversion from the war, as did the soldiers in the trenches who followed college football from afar. Other sports, such as major league baseball, offered diversion, but college football remained the only game in town for servicemen from south of the Mason-Dixon Line.

Despite Coach Aleck's opinion, there clearly were doubts that college football would be alive in 1943. In essence, the sport appeared to be on trial. The odds of everybody adapting to the change of circumstances seemed remote, and if things began to unravel, college football would likely be put on the shelf until the fighting overseas had run its course. Conversely, a successful college football season—one in which the games were exciting and the changes were viewed more as inconveniences than stumbling blocks—would go a long way toward keeping the sport alive for future wartime autumns.

Tech football had already begun to feel the sting of war firsthand. Bobby Beers, a wingback on the 1939 team that won the Orange Bowl, went into the U.S. Army Air Corps as a bomber pilot and died in an airplane accident in England in August. Burtz Boulware, a former Tech end, was killed in Texas during an accident at an army airfield, and Mickey Finn, a former Tech halfback, died when his parachute failed to open after he bailed out from a damaged plane.

The Auburn game loomed, but news from overseas never allowed thoughts of the war to leave anyone's consciousness for long. Still, Coach Aleck could take some comfort from letters like the one he received from Lieutenant R.W. "Buck" Murphy. Murphy, who had been a blocking back for Tech's 1940 Orange Bowl champions, wrote, "At this time of the year, most people start thinking about football and I am no exception even though I am a long way from it. I will miss seeing the games and will be pulling for Tech just as hard as if I were there."

Coach Aleck knew Murphy was serving in the European Theater, and the coach was well aware that 30 of the 33 players on that Orange Bowl championship squad were in the military.

The loss of loved ones and the unending absences of many others weren't the only ways in which the war impacted the home front. Staples such as butter, meat, and coffee were scarce, as were shoes and especially gas. Finding a metal appliance in the stores became a near impossibility. An all-for-one spirit continued to rally the country and could be seen, for example, in the rubber, scrap metal, and fat drives conducted by citizens across the country and in their enthusiastic investments in war bonds. "Rosie the Riveter" became a national symbol for women entering the workforce.

Diversions from the war included time spent on the dance floor, where jitterbugging was the rage. Any young man not wearing a military uniform would likely be wearing a zoot suit with a pronounced pleat in the pants and a long watch chain looped from pant waist to pocket. Girls favored saddle shoes, turned-down socks, and swirling skirts.

Castleberry had a nice smile with straight, white teeth, but he didn't much care for dancing and was strictly a one-woman man, despite his growing popularity. When asked about the opposite sex, Castleberry would quickly mention that the love of his life went to school at the Georgia State College for Women. Then he would add glowingly, "She's a queen."

Tech's squad began the 1942 season with just four starting seniors. Their first opponent, Auburn, was heralded to be much improved over a team that had made a strong finish to the 1941 season. Auburn was another microcosm of America's patriotism. Head Coach Jack Meagher had lost seven members of his coaching staff to the military, and the Marine Corps veteran intended to return to military service himself when the season ended. Many of Auburn's players planned to follow their coach's lead.

Bobby Dodd scouted the Tigers during their 20 – 7 win over Chattanooga the week before the Auburn – Tech game and spoke highly of the Tigers. "That Auburn outfit is not wearing round heels," Dodd said. "Rather I'd suggest they're equipped with spurs that go jingle-jangle. They're going to take a lot of stopping this season."

Keeping Castleberry under wraps likely influenced Coach Aleck to hold closed practices the week of the Auburn game. The few mentions of Castleberry in newspaper previews leading up to the game suggested that the freshman might see some action, but that was all. Castleberry's Boys' High career was probably responsible for those mentions. If Coach Aleck had had his way, Castleberry would not have been mentioned at all.

In contrast, Meagher didn't mind telling reporters about the experience of his players and the fact that they were the fastest team he had coached at Auburn. He told the press that he planned to run the T-formation and the Notre Dame Box behind a line heralded for its size. Meagher exuded confidence even though Tech had beaten the Tigers 28 – 14 in the previous year's meeting.

Oddly, Tech had exams the week of the game, which served as a distraction from the task at hand. At least one lineman and one back were said to be in danger of flunking out of school, and their futures hinged more on what happened in the classroom than what happened on the practice field. When the results were compiled, Davey Eldredge, who starred in the backfield, became one of the casualties and was declared ineligible for the Auburn game.

Even if Castleberry's name wasn't mentioned much in the media, the significance of having a freshman playing for Tech in the first game of the season wasn't lost on the newspapers. *The Atlanta Journal* pointed out that if Castleberry became the first freshman to enter the game for Tech, he would become the first to do so for the school since John Slaton had played, just after World War I had begun.

By the 3 P.M. kickoff time, the Tech – Auburn contest rated a toss-up to those wanting to place a wager on the outcome. The expected crowd of 18,000 would have been the largest opening-game crowd at Grant Field in years, but unfortunately for Tech, only 10,000 showed, in large part due to foul weather. Those who did attend were forced to open their umbrellas early in the contest. But the many restrictions that made attending a football game more difficult than ever before had caused a counterbalancing increase in radio audiences. Listening to the Tech game meant tuning into WGST, which stood for Georgia School of Technology.

The station had originated in 1922 as WBBF, a short-lived attempt by *The Atlanta Constitution* to compete with WSB, a station owned by rival newspaper *Atlanta Journal*. The following year, the *Constitution* gave WBBF to Georgia Tech, and the call letters became WGST. The station operated from the third floor of Georgia Tech's electrical engineering building in its early years but moved to the Ansley Hotel after being acquired by the Southern Broadcasting Company in 1930. It later moved to the Forsyth Building, from where it was broadcasting in 1942.

Those listening to Tech's first game of the 1942 season came away with the name Clint Castleberry burned into their ears. While Castleberry did not start, he entered the game quickly and peeled off a 5-yard scamper in his first collegiate carry. Wearing the number 19 on his jersey, he stood out in a game that depended largely on both teams' kick coverage and returns. When Tech punted, Castleberry repeatedly arrived to make a tackle just as the ball landed in the hands of Auburn's receiving man. Conversely, returning punts allowed him to display his swivel-hipped moves. He caught one punt on the run and returned the ball 30 yards, much to the delight of an adoring Atlanta crowd.

Though Castleberry did not score in Tech's 15 – 0 win, he led the running attack, successfully executing sweeps and off-tackle slants, and he played strong defense in addition to his work on punts. Coach Aleck would no longer be able to downplay the talents of his freshman sensation.

The Atlanta Journal ran a photograph of Castleberry running right to elude an Auburn tackler on the front page of its Sunday sports section. The headline for the caption read: "JACKRABBIT ON THE PROWL."

In the colorful language penned by columnist Jack Troy, Castleberry "darted, stopped, changed direction, darted some more and often galloped when given shirt tail distance on scrimmage plays."

Wrote Ed Miles of *The Atlanta Journal,* "Tech's Old Guard on the shelves of the West Stands hailed the freshman Castleberry as the fanciest runner to hit the Flats since they have forgotten when."

Immediately after Tech's win, the focus turned to their next opponent, Notre Dame. Tech would travel to South Bend the following weekend to play the Irish, who had managed only a 7 – 7 tie against Wisconsin in their first game. Most commentators predicted that Notre Dame's next opponent would pay for that tie, but at least one messenger wasn't so confident. When Notre Dame scout Wayne Millner reported back to Irish coach Frank Leahy on the Tech–Auburn game, he suggested that Castleberry was "the most dangerous runner in America." It was high praise for a freshman with just one college game under his belt.

11

On to South Bend

Coach Aleck dispatched Tech's travel squad to South Bend for the Notre Dame game on a Wednesday evening during the second week of the season. Castleberry—who obviously hadn't read his press clippings—acted surprised and elated to be on the list; he'd never traveled north of North Carolina prior to the trip.

On the day prior to departure, the entire Tech squad assembled on the grass of Grant Field to participate in a stretcher drill for the Red Cross in support of the war effort. After first-aid director W.W. Nealy described the technique to the players, groups of three moved a "robust" victim to a stretcher.

The drill served two purposes: first, to prepare the city for a possible air raid, and second, to advance the Red Cross's function of protecting the population against a natural catastrophe. Grant Field had been designated to serve as an air-raid shelter, a casualty station, and a first-aid post. The Red Cross publicized the drill hoping to inspire high school football players in the Atlanta area to volunteer for similar duty.

Red Cross chairman Oby Brewer observed the Tech team operate during the drills and came away favorably impressed. "This undoubtedly will be the best conditioned stretcher unit we'll have in the city of Atlanta," he said.

Helping to hold the players' attention were a pair of attractive nurses, which made being a practice patient in their care a welcome task.

According to an account in Murray Silver's *Tech's Luck*, Alexander gave his team an idea of what to expect when they got to Notre Dame, saying, "Men, when we get to South Bend, there'll be a big crowd to greet us. Bands will be playing, cheerleaders will be cheering, and the mayor will give us keys to the city. The people of South Bend will make the city ours, except for one thing they will reserve for themselves: the game."

On Thursday, 32 Georgia Tech players boarded a Southern Railroad train at Union Station to begin their trip to South Bend. Just prior to the train's scheduled departure, the train lost a Pullman that got redirected to an army troop, but the railroad scrambled and quickly found a comparable car, and the Tech team was on their way, traveling in the sleepers until they reached Cincinnati. Things got interesting in the River City. Since Tech's departure from Atlanta had been delayed, the team had roughly ten minutes to catch a transfer train to Chicago that was leaving from a platform approximately a quarter mile from where they disembarked. Bobby Dodd had been slow to rise and almost got left at the station. Later he observed, "I don't see how some of our slow tackles made it."

Players were expected to behave on the train and dress for the trip. "They made us present ourselves, not dressed to the nines, but we had to look pretty good," John Crawford said. "We didn't go up there with overalls on and that sort of thing. We dressed up."

The players passed time on the train primarily by playing cards. "Poker mainly," Crawford said. "You just got to know everybody better riding on the train. We weren't doing homework. No discussions of the game coming up or anything like that."

Castleberry had always had trouble sleeping on trains, dating back to the many train trips he had taken while playing for Boys' High. In lieu of slumber, he spent his time walking up and down the aisles or engaging in bull sessions with his teammates.

After reaching Chicago, the team caught a day coach back to South Bend. Despite the chaos of their journey, every member of the team and coaching staff arrived intact in South Bend at 3:30 Friday afternoon. Star Notre Dame running back Angelo Bertelli hadn't been as lucky the previous week; after catching the wrong train, he had not reached Madison until an hour before kickoff for the Wisconsin game.

Upon arrival, the Tech team quickly made its way to the Notre Dame campus for an afternoon workout, during which Castleberry experienced a moment of clarity about a play he thought would work against the Irish. Normally reserved and reticent, he boldly approached Coach Aleck to offer his thoughts. Most pass plays off sweeps were run to the right side because most backs threw the ball right-handed. Given that Castleberry threw left-handed, he suggested to Alexander that they run a pass to the left side. His coach seemed to consider the idea but said nothing to indicate he would try it. When a coach plans to try a different variation of a play in a game, he will normally have his offense execute the play in practice to gain a feel for it. That Coach Aleck chose not to dedicate any practice time to running the pass play to the left suggested that he wasn't embracing Castleberry's idea. When the practice concluded, the team went to its hotel for dinner before retiring for the evening.

Notre Dame had not lost a game in two years, and Tech had beaten them just once in the history of the rivalry, during Tech's 1928 national championship season, while the Irish had beaten Tech 11 times. Like a lot of other teams, Tech had never beaten the Irish at South Bend, and they had lost to Notre Dame 20 – 0 the previous year. Tech's chances against Notre Dame didn't look good.

Bertelli led the Notre Dame offense and carried a pedigree as one of the best players in the country. He had not performed well against Wisconsin, completing just four of 13 passes, which he attributed to having trouble spotting his receivers. That lackluster performance did not affect his confidence heading into the Tech game, however. He told reporters, "This is to give Tech fair warning not to forget what happened last year."

Tech's players took Bertelli's warning in stride and expressed confidence that they could rush Bertelli, as Wisconsin had done the previous week. Davey Eldredge would play for Tech after regaining his eligibility and earning a new nickname, "Eligible Eldredge." Oddsmakers rated Tech 20-point underdogs, but Frank

Leahy wasn't so confident. The coach of the Fighting Irish respected the speed of Tech's backs, and in scrimmages leading up to the game he worked his defense against Alexander's playbook of reverses, double reverses, and end-around plays. Leahy also warned Bertelli, who did the punting, to kick the ball away from the dangerous Castleberry.

Adding to the Castleberry hype were comparisons with former Tech running back Johnny Bosch, also a diminutive sort, who ran wild against the Irish in 1939 and nearly led an upset in Tech's eventual 17 – 14 loss.

Leahy came down with the flu, which caused him to cancel Friday afternoon's Irish workout. *The Atlanta Journal* reported that the Irish coach would try to make his return to the sideline by Saturday's game, speculating that if the doctor forbade him from attending, "he probably would ask his charges to play this one for their sick 'old man.' That would be bad for Tech as the Irish are a sentimental bunch."

Several factors did weigh in Tech's favor. First, Dippy Evans, Notre Dame's most dangerous runner, would not be available due to a knee injury. Next, most attributed Bertelli's less-than-stellar performance against Wisconsin to his discomfort throwing from the T-formation. In the previous year's win over Tech, Bertelli had appeared as if he could not miss a pass while throwing from the tailback spot in the single-wing formation. Nevertheless, Leahy changed the offense prior to the start of his second season as the Irish coach. In the single-wing formation, Bertelli took a long snap from the center much like the quarterback in a shotgun formation today, which allowed him more time to scan the field and look for his receivers. In the T-formation, however, he took the snap from under the center and then had to fade back while scanning the field.

Notre Dame Stadium sat south of Cartier Field, where the Irish had played their games until 1929. The new stadium had been built to accommodate the football team's immense success under coach Knute Rockne, who had coached at the new facility only during its inaugural season of 1930 before losing his life in a plane crash in 1931.

First-time visitors to Notre Dame Stadium could not help feeling in awe of the immense brick structure, which stood 45 feet high with a circumference of a half-mile and boasted a press box that towered 60 feet above the field. Well over 200 sportswriters could fit inside that structure, churning out copy on any given Saturday afternoon about what had transpired in the hub of college football.

Most in the crowd of 30,000 figured that Tech would be on the receiving end of retribution after Notre Dame's tie with Wisconsin. A win would affirm that the tie had been a fluke and the Irish merely had to scrape off some rust to regain their stately perch above the rest of college football.

Castleberry would be playing in just his second collegiate game in this intimidating setting. No doubt the freshman sensation had to tap into his past experiences at Boys' High just to buckle his chinstrap. Even a high school game of the highest standing could not have prepared Castleberry for playing the Irish at South Bend.

To a roar of the home crowd, Notre Dame ran onto the field resembling hulking giants in their dark gold pants and solid blue jerseys. Ten minutes later, Georgia Tech took the field wearing mustard-colored jerseys and white pants, looking every bit like undersized Christians about to be devoured by lions.

Leahy's warning about keeping punts away from Castleberry appeared to have spooked Bertelli. Mutt Manning partially blocked a slow-developing Bertelli punt in the second quarter, and Bertelli tried so hard to direct another punt away from Castleberry that he kicked the ball only 12 yards before it sailed out of bounds.

If Castleberry experienced any nervousness, he quickly overcame the feeling that afternoon in South Bend.

Midway through the third quarter of a scoreless game, Bertelli fumbled the football at the Notre Dame 28, and Castleberry recovered. Several plays later, Ralph Plaster plunged over from the 1-yard line for a touchdown. Tech still held a 7 – 0 lead in the fourth quarter when, for the first time, Bertelli punted to Castleberry and got burned accordingly. Castleberry tore off on an 18-yard return to start a Tech drive from the Irish 40.

Castleberry just had a knack for returning punts, according to Dwight Keith. "That was a thing of beauty, watching him return a punt," Keith said. "He never let the ball hit the ground, taking all kicks on the run. He had a lot of derring-do."

Bobby Dodd believed Castleberry's skills at fielding punts

stemmed from playing center field in baseball. "He judges a punt just like a fly ball. . . and he's never out of position," Dodd said. "Some backs—the poor ones—never do learn to judge a punt, and you'll find most times they never played baseball."

Tech found itself on the Notre Dame 8-yard line several plays after Castleberry's punt return. Coach Aleck knew his team could not squander the opportunity and needed a touchdown if they wanted to pull off the upset. Sensing the stop that would change the momentum, the Irish crowd grew louder. Unflustered, Castleberry got the call and tore off to the left side of the line on a sweep. After successfully sucking in the Notre Dame defense, which appeared to have hemmed him off from scooting into the end zone, Castleberry slammed on the brakes and cocked his arm. The southpaw normally didn't zip tight spirals. Rather, his passes arrived pillow-soft and easy to handle, and they always seemed to be on the money, too. Castleberry finished the play by throwing to a wide-open Pat McHugh in the end zone, triggering a collective moan from the home crowd. The freshman's second collegiate pass landed safely in McHugh's hands, leaving the Irish defenders looking dumb-founded while pushing Tech's lead to 13 – 0. The debut of the pass run to the opposite side—though unrehearsed—had been a glowing success.

Bob Miller began to get a sense of déjà vu at this point. Tech's line coach remembered being on the scene when Ohio State led Notre Dame 13 – 0 at the end of the third quarter during their 1935 tilt. The Irish cut the score to 13 – 12 with two quick scores before recovering a critical Ohio State fumble to take an unlikely come-from-behind 18 – 13 victory. Miller began to feel worse when Notre Dame stormed back to cut Tech's lead to 13 – 6. Tech needed either to kill the clock or score again. Such situations normally fall to players with the most experience, but this time Coach Aleck went again to Castleberry. He took the snap and held the football as if setting up to pass, but his arm never came forward. Instead, Tech wingback Jim Luck grabbed the ball while darting behind Castleberry and raced 40 yards thanks to a perfectly executed Statue of Liberty play. Notre Dame managed to put together another long drive in the game's final minutes before Manning intercepted at the Tech 27 to seal the Tech win.

The win against Notre Dame brought Dodd great joy. "Now we don't have to keep showing alumni those movies of our Orange Bowl game," he told Jack Troy of *The Atlanta Constitution*.

Dodd also seemed in awe of Castleberry. He later wrote in the *Saturday Evening Post* that Castleberry's performance "was almost stunning. Freshmen don't often beat Notre Dame."

Wayne Millner's warning to Leahy about Tech's first-year sensation had been prophetic. Castleberry's performance in such a high-profile arena, with major Midwest newspapers—including those from Chicago—covering the game and countless football fans listening on the radio, thrust him into the national spotlight. The perfect college football hero was born: a talented player who defined the American spirit by excelling despite his size.

"Comet" and "Jackrabbit" were among the nicknames sportswriters bestowed on Castleberry. Most of his teammates simply called him "C.D.," short for Clinton Dillard, or "Comic," a variation on Comet he earned during the train rides to and from South Bend. Several of the Tech players enjoyed passing the time by singing on the train. In particular they sang hymns, and according to Castleberry they sang pretty well, but when Castleberry tried to chime in, they told him he needed to keep quiet.

"They say I don't know one tune from another," said Castleberry, explaining that his teammates found his singing funny, which led to "Comet" becoming "Comic."

Tech enjoyed a lengthy layover in Chicago en route back to Atlanta, affording the team an opportunity to visit the aquarium and, later, a more risqué opportunity to attend a burlesque.

Atlanta's Union Station swelled with several thousand fans and Tech students to greet the Tech team upon their arrival home. An impromptu parade followed through the city streets, with the Tech band playing the school's fight song, "Ramblin' Wreck," along the way. There was a palpable hope in the air that Tech had embarked on a special season.

The Tech student body was further treated to a viewing of the game film at the gym, which led to raucous cheers, once again proving that a moment of triumph is no less fun to watch when the outcome is known.

A letter dated October 5, 1942, arrived at Coach Aleck's office the week after the Notre Dame game. It read:

> *Dear Bill:*
>
> *Just a few lines to let you know that, even though we lost the ball game last Saturday, we are happy in the thought that it was you and your club who handed us our defeat. Naturally, we hated to be beaten; but in losing to you, Coach, we feel we have lost to one of Notre Dame's time-honored friends.*
>
> *We think you have an excellent team and, if newspaper ink doesn't mean too much to them, you ought to finish your season undefeated. At least you have our fondest hopes for that goal.*
>
> *Please give my best to Bobby Dodd.*
>
> *Kindest regards.*
>
> *Sincerely yours,*
>
> *Frank Leahy*

12

Undefeated and Coach Aleck in Poor Health

Coach Aleck, though struggling with poor health, continued to be an outspoken advocate of maintaining college football during the war. He would enthusiastically defend the sport against those who believed the season should have been canceled. Richard J. Beamish, a public utility commissioner in Pennsylvania, could be counted among the numbers deeming college football unnecessary and a wasteful distraction for young men. The root of Beamish's zeal to condemn the sport seemed puzzling, since he had once coached football at St. Thomas College, a school that had since ceased to exist. Yet once the football season began he climbed onto a soapbox to argue that football needed to be put on the shelf until the end of the war and that all coaches should be relieved of their duties. Beamish further believed that school administrators were "derelict" in their jobs by allowing the "silly business of football" to stand in the way of wartime training, which needed to be taking place at the high school and college levels. Beamish's opinions received a national platform, which prompted Coach Aleck to weigh in on the subject.

"So he says he is a former athletic director and coach, does he?"

Coach Aleck told *The Atlanta Journal*. "Well, he probably was a poor man and lost his job.

"It seems to me that the football coaches are just as important as public utility commissioners at this time. I wonder what he is doing for the war? . . .I think Beamish just desires publicity. Being a politician, that is very natural for him."

As for the contribution of college football to military morale, letters such as this one to Ed Danforth, sports editor of *The Atlanta Journal*, from Private Edwin B. Lay, who was stationed in Fort Warren, Wyoming, were representative:

> *"I'm really a happy soldier now. All the fellows out here are mostly from the Middle West and the East. They were betting 2:1 that Georgia Tech would get beat by Notre Dame and I was taking them on at anywhere from 13 to 26 points. Boy, when old Tech came through for me, I was the happiest soldier in the Army! It really makes you feel good to know you've got something back home as good as any other state in the U.S.A. It's things like that that keep up morale while we are training to fight for peace. I'm from 1705 Mozley Drive, Atlanta."*

In October 1942, Reichsmarschall Hermann Goring, commander of the Luftwaffe and original head of the Gestapo, reaffirmed what the United States was fighting against when he announced that the war wasn't actually a "Second World War" but the "War of the Races." Several days later, President Roosevelt issued his own declaration against those guilty of wartime atrocities, vowing that they would be judged accordingly at the conclusion of the war. FDR's vow would be fulfilled in the Nuremberg Trials. Among the first 24 war criminals tried at Nuremberg was Goring. Found guilty of crimes against humanity and sentenced to death, he committed suicide the night before his execution.

On the home front in 1942, FDR embraced a new price control law in an effort to freeze wages, rents, and farm prices. The St. Louis Cardinals defeated the Yankees to take the World Series in five games, and Joe Louis announced his retirement from the ring. As with many champion fighters, Louis's retirement was later followed by a comeback.

In Atlanta, Coach Aleck wanted to make sure his team left the Notre Dame game back where they played it—in South Bend—as they looked forward to their next game against Chattanooga. Bobby Dodd wanted to keep Tech fans' expectations in check, too, which he attempted to do while speaking at the Atlanta Touchdown Club's weekly luncheon. Dodd reminded his audience that Notre Dame had been missing many of their top players, that several of the Irish's top players had not been up to form, and that Tech had taken advantage of several breaks, yet the Irish had still taken the game down to the wire. He summed up by noting that the Tech coaching staff had no illusions about the team being invincible.

The Chattanooga game kicked off at 3 P.M. on October 10 at Grant Field and was billed as "Bargain Day," with tickets available for $1.65. Twelve thousand fans showed up to watch Tech win 30 – 12 and remain undefeated for the season.

A poignant moment took place at halftime when the Tech band played "The Tech Victory Song," which had been written by Jimmy Beers and dedicated to his late brother Bobby, the former Tech player who had enlisted in the army air corps and died in an airplane accident in England two months earlier. The song was another reminder that the country was at war and nobody knew who would be alive afterward.

Castleberry played just one quarter, scoring two touchdowns, including what one sportswriter called "one of the most amazing runs ever seen on Grant Field." Dropping back to pass, he saw that nobody was open and instead scooted around the right side for a 26-yard score. He also showed off his arm more than in the previous two games, impressing observers with his accuracy.

Veteran sportswriter Ed Miles of *The Atlanta Journal* wrote that "Clint Castleberry was a crazed jackrabbit. . . . He twisted and squirmed out of grips, bounced off shoulders, spun out of arms, running all the while to an individual glory not won by a Tech man since Everett Strupper." Strupper had been a standout running back on Tech's 1917 national championship team.

Not counting kickoffs or points after touchdowns, the two teams ran 159 plays from scrimmage, ten plays more per quarter than normal. Coach Aleck pointed out that a lot of passes were thrown, stopping the clock on many occasions. Still, the game lasted just 2 hours 7 minutes, an amazing contrast to the lengthy televised college football games of decades later, punctuated by commercial breaks.

In Mississippi, Frankie Sinkwich and Charlie Trippi ran wild in leading Georgia to a 48 – 13 rout of Ole Miss to remain undefeated on the season.

When the weekly rankings came out, Ohio State, led by legendary coach Paul Brown, held the top spot in the Associated Press poll. Georgia was ranked second, followed by Michigan, Alabama, Illinois, and Georgia Tech. Suddenly, Coach Aleck and Bobby Dodd were under consideration to coach in the prestigious Blue-Gray football game the day after Christmas.

Unknown to most, however, Coach Aleck was suffering from a disease of the gall bladder in addition to having a heart condition and a prostate problem that often forced him to lean against goalposts during practices. When he struck that familiar pose, everybody knew Coach Aleck was urinating. Heeding a warning from his doctors, Alexander stayed away from work from October 11 through 17, allowing Dodd to run the team through its paces in advance of Tech's next game against Davidson. After Davidson, the schedule would take a treacherous turn; Tech would conclude their 1942 season against Navy, Duke, Kentucky, Alabama, Florida, and Georgia.

Dodd's practices were similar to those run by Coach Aleck, seeking a high level of execution through repetition. But Dodd wasn't Coach Aleck. He carried with him a playfulness that "the Old Man" lacked, due largely to the fact he was not as far removed from his playing years as his mentor and boss. In many of the players' minds, "Dodd" was a four-letter synonym for fun.

"Bobby Dodd would get out there and play touch football with us," Joe Daniel said. "He'd be on one team, and if your team beat him, he'd buy you a milkshake. He could still get around back then. They wanted to make it enjoyable. It was fun to play at Tech. We worked hard, but we still had little things like that. That's how they worked."

Nobody would bet against Dodd when he proposed a wager based on his drop-kicking abilities.

"He could drop-kick a ball anywhere," Daniel said. "At indoor practice, he'd drop-kick the ball toward the basketball goal and darn near put it through the nets. He just exuded confidence."

Dodd's relaxed approach included instituting volleyball games during the light Friday workouts. Improvising, they used a football for a volleyball and a goalpost crossbar as the net. A born competitor, Dodd also played golf and poker for higher stakes than milkshakes.

Many had forecast that the 1942 college football season would be unpredictable, and that forecast began to unfold early in the season. Florida's 6 – 0 win over highly favored Auburn the previous week served as proof of how volatile things were.

After beating Auburn, Notre Dame, and Chattanooga in successive games, Tech players might have been tempted to view little regarded Davidson as a mere respite before heading off to Annapolis to play Navy. If ever a team were primed for an upset, Georgia Tech was. Several key players were nursing minor injuries, and Dodd would be filling in for Coach Aleck. Though Dodd had served a long apprenticeship, he had not yet made his bones as a head coach. A sloppy practice during the week added grist to the notion that a Dodd-coached Tech team could fall from its lofty perch.

Inspiration for Tech came from an unlikely source, Davidson head coach Gene McEver. For some reason, McEver felt compelled to state Davidson's case by making what was, for the time, a cocky statement.

"Davidson always has been known as an upset team and we fight harder and play better when we're up against somebody big," said McEver in an Associated Press story. "We're going to Atlanta to give Georgia Tech a ball game."

McEver broke a cardinal rule of football: Never awaken a sleeping giant.

Davidson did manage to hold down Castleberry. Their defensive game plan from the outset was obviously to stop him, and their efforts paid off as he gained just 16 yards on eight carries. But concentrating on the "Jackrabbit" permitted the rest of Tech's offense to run wild. Tech never allowed Davidson to scent an upset, defeating their guests 33 – 0 in front of 11,000 fans at Grant Field. Coach Aleck watched from the sideline like a spectator while Dodd called the shots.

Suddenly football in the Southeastern Conference resembled a three-horse race between undefeated teams: Tech, Georgia, and Alabama. Based on the composition of their team and the remaining games on their schedule, Georgia became the odds-on favorite to finish the season without a blemish. Tech and Alabama looked like Georgia's only potential stumbling blocks. Alabama, with upcoming games against Kentucky, Georgia, Tech, and Vanderbilt, seemed likely to finish just behind Georgia, while Tech had the toughest remaining schedule with games against Navy, Duke, Kentucky, Alabama, and Georgia. The scenario that would see all three teams face one another became known as "the round-robin of Dixie." Georgia and Alabama were scheduled to play in Atlanta— a location chosen due to wartime travel restrictions—on October 31, while Tech would play Alabama in Atlanta on November 14 and Georgia in Athens on November 28. All three teams knew that an undefeated passage would likely mean a Rose Bowl invitation with a shot at winning the national championship.

Castleberry, though thwarted against Davidson, had established himself as the top freshman player in the country, but other freshmen were making impacts. On successive Saturday afternoons, Princeton's freshman fullback George Franke scored the winning touchdown against Navy and the tying touchdown against Penn. Boston College featured triple-threat freshman back Bill Boyce, Georgia had 179-pound fullback Sonny Lloyd, and Florida counted Billy Mims as one of the team's top backs. The performances of these freshmen shot down one of the major arguments against freshman eligibility made by the Big Ten, Pacific Coast, Southwest, and Southern Conferences, all of whom believed that freshmen would be outmanned against upper-class competition.

Fox Movietone News featured the Tech – Notre Dame game in its weekly production shown before the movies. And when the Williamson system rankings were released on October 20, Tech had risen to third in the country behind Alabama and Georgia. The Associated Press ranked Tech sixth in the nation as the team prepared for what looked like its biggest hurdle to date, in Annapolis against the Naval Academy Midshipmen. Already sportswriters were calling Tech a "team of destiny."

13

Anchors Away

Navy's storied football program had produced a national championship in 1926 and consistently fielded high-caliber teams. Georgia Tech had not played the Midshipmen since 1922, a game Tech had lost 13 – 0.

Navy had gone 7 – 1 – 1 in 1941, but the Midshipmen had lost a lot of good players, the classes of 1942 and 1943 having graduated early due to the war. After four games in the fall of 1942, Navy stood at 2 – 2, having lost to Princeton and William & Mary while defeating Virginia and Yale. More to the point, however, Navy appeared to be improving quickly, and they carried a winning attitude from the previous year. They might be a young team, but playing them in Annapolis presented a formidable challenge for Tech.

Most of the football Tech had played to that point in the season had been played in rain, which created muddy field conditions and limited Tech's particular strengths: quickness and the passing game. Good weather was expected for the clash with Navy, which added a measure of confidence for Tech.

Tech possessed a deep stable of running backs, yet the freshman from Boys' High had been stealing the show from his talented older running mates. Bob Sheldon, who was one of those backs, pointed out that Castleberry's standing wasn't a fluke.

"He was head and shoulders above all of us," Sheldon said. "He had no trouble with the college game. He was so unusual. He was a natural. And he was a very deceptive runner. He had good legs, strong legs, speed and quickness. I'll say this, he could play today, and there aren't many of us I could say that about. He was well built for his size."

Understanding the weapon they had in Castleberry, Coach Aleck and Bobby Dodd continued to seek more ways to get him involved in the offense.

"One of the plays they put in was unique and just for Clint because it took advantage of his quickness," Joe Daniel said. "He was so quick, they'd block like he was going to the right and he'd go to the left—what you'd call a misdirection play. He'd be gone before the defense even reacted. He was that quick and fast, and deceptive too."

The Georgia Tech–Navy game received considerable attention. It matched two tradition-laden football schools that rarely met, and Tech would be putting its undefeated season on the line. NBC and CBS were scheduled to broadcast the game in the United States, and the Armed Forces Radio Network would be broadcasting it to troops around the world.

Tech arrived at Atlanta's Union Station on Thursday afternoon uncertain about their travel arrangements, given the national restrictions on transportation. If all went well, the team would travel on the Southern Railroad and arrive in Annapolis in time for a Friday afternoon workout at Thompson Stadium. A little uneasiness always accompanied any effort to transport college kids from one destination to another, and wartime uncertainty added a little spice to the Tech administrators' anxiety. All went well until the train stopped in Baltimore, just short of Annapolis. At that point several players got off the train, and they had not returned by the time the train started the final leg of its journey.

"We got off the train to look around the city some," John Crawford said. "We were just out looking at the town and maybe trying to find out what the feminine gender of Baltimore looked like. There were five of us, and Clint was one. The train started off and we weren't on it. All I know is we saw the train going and it went up the tracks for a little bit before it started backing up. They had to back it up because they couldn't go play Navy without their star. He was that good. They backed the train up to pick up Castleberry, and on our way to Annapolis we went."

By game day, most pundits, including esteemed columnist Grantland Rice, had picked Tech as the favorite. Hoping to will their way to an upset, Navy pulled out all their good-luck charms. Melissa the "Meddlesome Mutt" led the team onto the field in front of a crowd of 22,000 at Thompson Stadium. Melissa had not been at the William & Mary game and had not traveled to the Princeton game, so neither of Navy's two losses could be tagged on the lucky canine. Melissa's specific instructions were to hex the Tech squad. In addition, the Midshipmen employed "Old Bill IV," their goat mascot, as well as Tecumseh, a lucky statue.

Tech took the field in their mustard-colored jerseys, while Navy wore bright gold pants with dark blue jerseys. Lending a regal feeling to the atmosphere were the scrambled eggs, gold stars, and eagles adorning the uniforms of the high brass from all branches of the military who were sitting in the stands. A cold breeze punctuated the air, forcing most in the crowd to wear overcoats or huddle under blankets.

Castleberry began the day with a 31-yard jaunt around end that served notice to the partisan Navy crowd that he was not some flash-in-the-pan newspaper creation. Both teams threatened in the first quarter, but neither scored. Early in the second quarter, Navy mounted a modest drive after recovering a punt fumbled by Tech's Eddie Prokop at the Navy 45. The Midshipmen advanced the ball to the Tech 29, where the Tech defense stiffened to force a fourth-and-long situation.

Navy sat just outside field goal range, but they weren't about to punt so deep in Tech territory. Knowing the situation called for a pass, Coach Aleck inserted Castleberry into the game, instructing the explosive little playmaker to make an interception.

One play can define an athlete, one moment in which every movement falls into place and, for a fleeting instant, the athlete attains perfection. Such plays elevate athletics from human striving—noble in itself—to a momentary state of grace, capturing the

imaginations and memories of witnesses. Legions of Clint Castleberry fans were born shortly after the Wee Jackrabbit ran onto the
field, leaving Coach Aleck standing on the Tech sideline.

Navy tailback Al Cameron took the snap at the right hash
mark and set up to throw toward the end zone. Like most great
athletes, Castleberry possessed a keen awareness of where the ball
was at all times, and this play was no exception. Recognizing the
direction of Cameron's pass, Castleberry broke for the ball, step-
ping in front of the Navy receiver at the 5-yard line to snatch the
pass from midair at the last instant. Then the Jackrabbit's magic
took over.

While 22,000 football fans watched from the stands, a large
radio audience was glued to the action from coast to coast in the
United States and throughout the European and Pacific theaters. A
radio play-by-play is a blank canvas on which the listener's imagination paints details. Here is what listeners heard:

> *Second quarter, still 0 – 0. Navy in an obvious passing sit-
> uation. Long pass. Intercepted by Castleberry at the Tech 5. . . .*

A roar of crowd noise followed. Navy had been knocking on
the door to score the first points of the game, and suddenly the partisan Navy crowd was pleading for one of the Middies' eleven to
put a stop to the return.

While securing the ball, Castleberry made a lateral cut to his
left to elude the intended receiver, then broke back across the field
to his right at an angle toward the sideline, switching the ball to his
right hand as he went to avoid a strip. Great backs can see daylight and recognize where an opening is about to develop, and
Castleberry possessed that ability. At the Tech 30 he darted back
toward the middle of the field, and suddenly he was in open space.
Harvey Hardy made a tremendous block against the final Navy
defender at midfield, and by the time Castleberry stopped running
he had crossed into the Middies' end zone for a 95-yard touchdown.

"That run was a thing of beauty," Crawford said. "Nobody had
ever seen anything like it."

Dodd threw his fedora down on the ground and grabbed

Castleberry as the entire Tech sideline celebrated the play. In stark contrast, Navy looked deflated.

"I had no idea when I caught that pass that I'd get anywhere," said Castleberry later in a United Press International interview. "But I picked up some good blocking . . . and not a man touched me."

By the end of Tech's 21 – 0 rout, Castleberry had added three batted-down passes to end Navy scoring threats and made an electrifying 51-yard run on the final play of the game.

Dodd later called the interception return against Navy Castleberry's "greatest" play, offering his own description of it: "Near the end of a scoreless first half, the Middies marched to our 20-yard line with blood in their eyes. They flipped a pass right to the goal line. Clint intercepted it and ran it back the entire length of the field for a touchdown—a magnificent run that I can still follow step by step in my mind. It shook Navy to its keel, and Tech won, 21 – 0."

Sheldon remembered a bizarre scene in the Tech dressing room after the game, with "Navy brass, several admirals, and captains" beating on the Tech door to talk to Castleberry. "They collared Clint and wanted to sign him up for the Naval Academy, so he could play ball up there," Sheldon said. And the Naval Academy might have gotten their way except that Castleberry had already signed up for the army air corps.

Equally enamored with Castleberry were the young boys of Atlanta, who listened to his exploits on the radio and dreamed of becoming football heroes themselves. Franklin Cullen "Pepper" Rodgers of Atlanta, a precocious 10-year-old, could be counted among that number. Already a self-avowed sports junkie, Rodgers listened to all of Tech's games on WGST. Reading the newspapers, he saw all the posed pictures in which Castleberry would jump into the air for the photographer as if to throw a left-handed pass.

"I spent a lot of hours behind the school learning how to throw left-handed and jumping up in the air like they did at that time," Rodgers said. "I'm ambidextrous because of Clint Castleberry. He was a real hero of mine."

Radio accounts such as those from the Navy game only served to enhance Castleberry's image for a huge listening audience. "When you listened on the radio, he could be anything you wanted him to be," Rodgers said. "That's the magic of radio. You make them out what you want them to be."

So the legend grew.

Reviews of the Navy game thrust Castleberry into the national limelight. The report in *The Washington Post* asked why the Eastern press hadn't "heard of this fine player prior to the Navy game."

Meanwhile, Georgia continued to look imposing, throttling previously unbeaten Cincinnati 35 – 13. Alabama took care of Kentucky 12 – 0. The three Southeastern Conference frontrunners remained unbeaten.

14

Duke and the Rest of the Field

Georgia Tech feared that Duke would be their toughest opposition since the Notre Dame game. The two schools had begun playing in 1933, and Tech had won just twice while losing seven times to the Blue Devils. Durham had been a graveyard for Tech. In the history of the rivalry, no Tech football team had left the Duke campus with a victory. And if history wasn't enough to cast the outcome into doubt, Duke entered the game fresh off a dominating 28 – 0 win over a good Pittsburgh team.

O.B. Keeler of *The Atlanta Journal* wrote before the game that Duke had "had a habit of drubbing Georgia Tech . . . for some time."

In the week before the game, Castleberry's eligibility was in question. While the Southeastern Conference had made freshmen eligible, Duke played in the Southern Conference, which had not. (Duke would leave the Southern Conference in 1953 to join Maryland, North Carolina, South Carolina, Clemson, North Carolina State, and Wake Forest as a charter member of the fledgling Atlantic Coast Conference.) Earlier that season, Colgate had been denied the use of its freshmen against Duke even though freshmen were eligible in Colgate's conference. In the end, the issue came down to paperwork. Colgate had one type of contract for their game against Duke, while Tech had another. Duke authorities answered a query about the matter with a letter stating, "While we as a conference, and as individuals, are not permitted to play freshmen, our contract with Tech is clear. The responsibility of interpreting eligibility rests with them."

According to Tech's way of thinking, Castleberry was eligible.

Tech planned to leave for Durham at 8 P.M. on the Thursday before the game, hoping to reach their destination at a reasonable time. Concerned about wartime transportation restrictions, and knowing that Durham was relatively inaccessible by train, Bobby Dodd haggled with the railroads about Tech's travel arrangements, particularly the final 26 miles between Raleigh and Durham.

Duke hoped to extend their winning streak over Tech to eight games and felt confident about doing so, which might explain why the Blue Devils had scheduled Tech for their homecoming game.

Blue Devils coach Eddie Cameron didn't believe that Duke held a jinx over Tech, though. "I've never heard of a jinx making a tackle yet," he said, and added, "But if there is such a thing, we certainly can use it, or him, in that game tomorrow. At right tackle to be specific."

After Duke's scout team ran the Tech offense with great success against his starting defense, Cameron expressed disappointment in his defense's ability to do anything against the myriad of formations run from the single-wing. The spinning and ball handling in the backfield made sorting out who had the ball a particularly difficult proposition. Further anxiety for Cameron came in the realization that a scout team could never adequately simulate the speed and athleticism of another school's starting offense.

Tech's game, while significant for Tech, paled in comparison to the game taking place in Atlanta: the first game of the so-called round-robin of Dixie, pitting Alabama against Georgia at Grant Field. The loser of the game would be at a distinct disadvantage to finish the season with a bowl game or top national ranking. Alabama's defense could not be scored upon, and Georgia's offense could not be stopped. It would be an outstanding match-up.

Castleberry's magic, Tech's two games in Northern venues, and Frankie Sinkwich's marquee value had all prompted the national press—which was heavily weighted toward the Northeast—to tune in to Southern football. Even noted *Washington Post* columnist Shirley Povich offered his two cents about Castleberry, writing, "If it weren't for the long-held prejudices against quick recognition of young upstarts, that lad Clint Castleberry might well be the first freshman in decades to win All-American rating. He's the boy in the Georgia Tech backfield who completed one of Navy's passes at Annapolis Saturday and toted it 95 dazzling yards to a touchdown."

Tech arrived in Durham on Friday afternoon as hoped, in time for a 4 o'clock workout at Duke Stadium, where a freshman game between Duke and North Carolina State had just ended. Keeler's observations of that practice typified the hometown booster reporting of the era. "I was glad to note," he wrote, "that our brave boys, loping out of their own boudoir for the practice, looked a good deal larger in uniform than in their civvies or regular clothes."

A familiar scenario began to unfold when the Blue Devils took a 7 – 0 lead early in the game. All of the demons of Tech – Duke football history seemed present, bringing to roaring life the crowd of 30,000 that filled the horseshoe-shaped stadium. Unfortunately for Duke, the lead and the jinx failed to register with Castleberry. The freshman took over the game, making what were described as "impossible runs" against a huge Duke line. Castleberry turned in his typical all-around game, passing the ball well and returning kicks with unparalleled gusto. By game's end he had returned five kicks for 200 yards and intercepted a pass to lead Tech to a 26 – 7 win.

Tech's win over Duke kept the Yellow Jackets undefeated through six games, while Georgia managed a come-from-behind win over Alabama.

Georgia fell behind 10 – 0 before storming back to score 21 points in the fourth quarter. The game featured hard hitting on both sides of the ball, but Georgia's conditioning appeared to be the biggest factor late in the game. Wally Butts, though considered a son of a bitch by detractors, had always been a stickler for conditioning. Behind the countless windsprints and rules about not smoking, Butts had a plan. Having the best-conditioned team in the fourth quarter paid rich dividends, and never had this been more evident than during Georgia's furious fourth-quarter comeback.

Sinkwich hooked up on passes to George Poschner for two of the Bulldogs' touchdowns. Sinkwich's old Youngstown, Ohio schoolmate—who had received a scholarship to Georgia thanks to Sinkwich—had developed into an All-American end. He possessed soft hands on offense and a punishing tackling style on defense.

Some 33,000 fans at Grant Field remained in their seats to the end, wondering if Alabama could mount a final comeback. But Georgia salted the game away with a fumble recovered in midair and returned for a touchdown. According to college rules at the time, the ball could not have been advanced if it had been recovered after hitting the ground.

Following the game, the hard-assed Butts showed a softer side. Tears streamed down his chubby cheeks as the Georgia coach declared, "I'm so happy, I don't know what to say."

Georgia's victory thrust them into the top spot of the Associated Press poll on November 3, while Wisconsin, which had tied Ohio State, moved to second and Tech went to third. Anticipation for the November 28 contest between Tech and Georgia had already begun.

A local writer figured that Georgia had the best chance of facing Tech with a clean slate. He calculated the odds at 10 to 1 in favor of Georgia finishing the season undefeated, while the "awesome finishing section of the Tech schedule" made Tech's chances of heading to Athens undefeated only 50:50.

Talk continued across the country about the impact of keeping college football going, and how doing so helped the war effort. At a Chicago Quarterback Club luncheon at the Morrison Hotel in downtown Chicago, Major John L. Griffith reported his findings on the subject by contrasting the armies of Germany and the United States. Griffith noted that the Germans had relied on physical training, drilling, and calisthenics during World War I, while the majority of U.S. soldiers had some background in sports, which led to "individual initiative, self-reliance, and an ability to take command and make decisions." Griffith emphasized that the American way paid off particularly when an officer got wounded or killed in battle, as American enlisted men had an easier time taking command than their German counterparts.

15

Dodd Takes Over

Tech remained undefeated, but the Duke game had exacted a great physical toll on the team. Castleberry could be counted among the wounded after aggravating an old high-school shoulder injury. Nine of Tech's 22 starters were so banged up that they could not practice until Wednesday, just three days prior to the next game against Kentucky.

Of even graver concern, Coach Aleck's heart condition had intensified. He suffered what was reported to be a coronary occlusion that was complicated by his gall bladder ailment. Behind the scenes, only a select few knew that Coach Aleck had suffered a heart attack. His doctor ordered him to take two weeks of bed rest, which left Dodd at the helm for Tech's games against Kentucky and Alabama.

"It seems the M.D.'s think I was fortunate to get by the Duke and Navy games without a collapse," Alexander said. "But two weeks in bed and a diet will fix me up."

Dodd was more than prepared and had the talent to execute the plays he chose to run. Seemingly, his time had come. Though he'd been on the job since his eligibility had run out at Tennessee, he looked younger than his years, save for a misshapen segment on the bridge of his nose. Since facemasks were not yet a part of the football helmet, most assumed that the flaw in his features had been created on the football field. Actually, though, he had incurred the injury in a basketball game between Tennessee and Georgia Tech in Atlanta.

Dodd loved telling the story of how Vance Maree had done a number on his nose. The fun-loving coach always began the anecdote by complimenting Maree's football talents and noting that he had been a tackle on Tech's Rose Bowl championship team. But, Dodd would then add, Maree's talents did not extend to the hardwood.

Dodd played guard for Tennessee, and when he tried to move past Maree an elbow found his nose, sending him "off on queer street for a minute or two." A doctor stuffed Dodd's nose with cotton, and he continued to play. Tennessee won the game, but shortly after Dodd got showered and dressed, the pain in his nose began to bother him. Thinking that blowing his nose might relieve the pain, he did so, and out came a piece of bone. The side of his nose collapsed on one side, and there was no surgery at the time that could put the bone back in place. Dodd relished the irony in the story, always noting that he had finished his football career injury-free.

While evolving into a fine head-coach-in-waiting during his apprenticeship, Dodd had also adopted many of Coach Aleck's philosophies about student athletes. Coach Aleck believed that every player should attain his college degree while playing football at Georgia Tech, and so did Dodd. Dodd had never worked hard in school, and despite attaining star athletic status at Tennessee, he had never graduated. He had since grown to regret that and always tried to pass along his feelings to the Tech players.

One definite difference between Dodd and Coach Aleck likely stemmed from the fact that Dodd had been a player of great athletic ability, whereas Coach Aleck had not.

"Dodd had been a very successful ballplayer at Tennessee and Coach Aleck had been a scrub at Tech," Bob Sheldon said. "And their approach to the players seemed to be just the opposite. Dodd appreciated effort and someone who competed, while Coach Aleck was just the opposite. He cared more about a player's talent and reputation.

"I didn't have a hell of a lot of speed and all, but I had desire. Dodd, I think, appreciated that more than Coach Aleck. If Coach Aleck did, he never said or did anything to indicate that. I admired Coach Aleck, but I just thought Dodd could do no wrong."

Though Dodd had not yet advanced to head coach status—other than being an interim in Coach Aleck's absence—he had already mastered the poor-mouthing routine that was practically second nature to Southern coaches. Prior to the game with Kentucky, he told reporters, "Kentucky may be on the verge of breaking out all over Grant Field with their best game of the year. They can give us fits unless we are at our best."

Few believed that Tech would struggle with Kentucky, even if Georgia had only beaten the Wildcats by a score of 7 – 6. Instead, most looked past Kentucky to Tech's meeting with Georgia in Athens on November 28, figuring that both schools might be undefeated entering that game. Tickets for the Tech – Georgia contest were already becoming scarce; reports of the game being close to selling out were circulating the week of Tech's contest against Kentucky. Tickets for a Tech or Georgia game could usually be purchased at department stores in downtown Atlanta, but those stores were already sold out for the November 28 game. In addition, Tech's athletic office reported that all of their allotted seats had been sold, and that left only end zone seats, which had to be purchased from Georgia.

Dodd planned to give the offense a thorough prepping for the Kentucky defense, and he began by giving the varsity the day off on the Monday prior to the game. Not only did the varsity *need* a day off—having practiced or played every day since September 1— but their absence allowed Dodd to give his full attention to the third-stringers, prepping them to offer a reasonable facsimile of the Wildcat formations when they began lining up against the Tech varsity at practice the following day.

Having been a quarterback and now the offensive brain of the Yellow Jackets, Dodd felt that the battle waged between the two sides in a football game remained in a constant state of flux, with each side adjusting to the other to gain an advantage. If the opponent came up with a successful strategy for stopping an offensive formation, the coach's primary imperative was to figure out a way around this before having to take a loss to do so. Often he would find the solution after scrutinizing films from his team's previous game to determine what plays the other team's defense had been successful in stopping and what they were doing to be successful. Dodd made the whole process sound simple, noting that he let the other team do the work for him. His persona radiated a sense of ease and fun, which was likely just a facade for all the work he did behind the scenes.

While Castleberry highlighted the list of the injured and did not practice all week, fellow backfield mate Eddie Prokop had a wisdom tooth extracted, and several of the linemen were suffering from knee injuries. Given the inexact science of diagnosing joint trauma at the time, the severity of those injuries was unknown.

In contrast, Kentucky reported being healthy for the first time since they had lost to Georgia, which meant that star Wildcat running back Phil Cutchin would be in the lineup. Kentucky would have tied Georgia and Vanderbilt had their kicker not missed extra points, and they had been engaged in a scoreless tie with Alabama until Cutchin got injured, which opened the door for the Crimson Tide to take a 14 – 0 win.

Ab Kirwan wasn't about to concede any advantage to his team even if Tech's whole squad had been reported injured. By midweek the Kentucky coach had moved into full Southern coach-speak, building up Tech and talking hangdog about his own team. He also managed a few poorly cloaked shots at his old rival Wally Butts, calling Tech a better team than Georgia. According to Kirwan, the Bulldogs' greatest asset was their good fortune to have Frankie Sinkwich wearing one of their uniforms. "Georgia is a great team, there's no question about that," he said, "but Frankie Sinkwich makes the Bulldogs great. Take that astute aerial artist out of the game and Georgia is but a 'good' team."

Kirwan added, "I can't see where Georgia gets the nod over Tech as the country's outstanding team."

Statistics offered a strong counterbalance to Kirwan's opinion about Georgia. According to the American Football Statistical Bureau, Georgia entered that week's game against Florida averaging 412.9 yards a game, an extraordinarily high total for the era and a testament to Sinkwich's abilities and Butts's understanding of the passing game.

Bowl talk accompanied the early November contests. The coming 1943 bowl season would include the Orange, Sugar, Cotton, and Rose bowls. Unlike the bowl season that would evolve by the end of the century, all of the games—save for an occasional minor bowl game—were played on New Year's Day, which made going to a bowl game rare and special. Tech appeared to be earmarked for an appearance in the Sugar Bowl against Boston College. Meanwhile, the Rose Bowl might once again be played in Pasadena, and if transportation arrangements would allow one of the Southern heavyweights to make the trip, West Coast papers were touting the merits of a Georgia – UCLA contest.

But Dodd didn't want his players to think about bowl games. He reminded them that Kentucky needed to be dealt with in order for any bowl talk to continue.

By game time on Saturday, Tech's outlook appeared brighter, as eight of the team's nine injured players—including Castleberry—were suited up and ready to play, though their playing times were likely to be limited. As things turned out, however, playing times were a moot point.

Tech took a 47 – 7 win despite Dodd's efforts to hold down the score. Believing that "what goes around, comes around," he used 37 players during the contest, including some so obscure their names were omitted from the program. The points just continued to mount.

Castleberry shone again, despite nursing the injury from the Duke game. He broke four tackles en route to a 40-yard touchdown run and scored another from 25 yards out on a fake pass.

"He's a hard runner and elusive—runs with his feet well apart—and is hard to knock down," Dodd said. "He jerks away from tacklers like a big back would do." Dodd would later say that he could think of no other back with whom to compare Castleberry, "for his bowlegged style was that different." Dodd felt that Castleberry was special as a safety man as well, due to his expertise at "two of the toughest jobs in football, catching punts and defending against passes."

The more Dodd saw of Castleberry, the more he admired the youngster's demeanor as much as his ability.

"He doesn't talk much, except when you speak first," Dodd said. "He's polite, and takes instructions on the jump. All the boys like him."

Dodd believed that all natural athletes never got nervous. Having been a gifted and natural athlete himself, Dodd understood the advantage of being able to play a game without being nervous. Castleberry possessed that trait, and Dodd knew it.

"Before he came to Tech he made a great record at Boys' High," Dodd said. "Many people doubted he would be able to play that kind of ball here. But instead of being nervous, he's the calmest, most conservative back on the squad."

Dodd had done just fine while pinch-hitting for Coach Aleck. Nobody could have foreseen Tech's total dismantling of Kentucky, which came on the same day that 100,000 American troops landed in North Africa under the direction of Dwight Eisenhower and George Patton. Away from the action at Grant Field, Coach Aleck remained true to his word. He stayed at home on the advice of his doctor and didn't even know the final score until his maid woke him from an afternoon nap. Upon hearing the news, Coach Aleck smiled, then drifted back to sleep.

Dodd, Castleberry, and company might have received even more publicity for their rout had Georgia not beaten Florida 75 – 0. Sinkwich ran for two touchdowns and threw two more to George Poschner to lead the Bulldogs to their fourteenth consecutive win dating back to the middle of the 1941 season. Famed journalist and humorist Arthur "Bugs" Baer wrote, "Nobody's marching through Georgia these days." In the aftermath of the Tech and Georgia wins, the two teams went to the top of the Associated Press and Williamson polls, with Georgia first and Tech second. But rankings meant little to Georgia Tech. Lurking on the horizon was the second game of the round-robin of Dixie, the game against an Alabama team that was still smarting from their lone defeat against Georgia.

16

Crimson Tide Crossroads

Despite the distance separating Clint Castleberry and Shirley Poole, their courtship continued in the fall of 1942. During the week they would communicate by mail. Castleberry wrote long, thoughtful letters informing his girl about the week's events and everything going on in his life. Corresponding through the mail wasn't unusual then; long-distance telephone calls were costly enough to be taboo for any college student's budget.

On Friday afternoons Poole would head to the Greyhound station in Milledgeville to board a bus for the 2 ½-hour ride to Atlanta. Castleberry would pick her up at the Atlanta station, and if Tech had a game the next day they might get a bite to eat before he took her to her parents' house.

On Saturdays she attended the Tech games even though she knew little about football, a fact she attributed to being an only child and not having any brothers or sisters to "coach" her on the sport early in her life. "I wasn't too interested in football," Shirley said. "But I guess I liked the idea of being with a celebrity to a certain degree."

Shirley's beauty and her status as a football hero's girlfriend prompted her to get "sponsored" on more than one occasion. When sponsored for a game, her duties called for her to wear a pretty dress, hold a bouquet of flowers, and smile broadly. She was, in short, on display. Like her boyfriend, Shirley lacked height, which prompted her to wear her hair "tall."

Though she didn't understand football, she did understand that it involved violent collisions. Her boyfriend had good size for a jackrabbit but not for a major college football player, so any such collisions could bring undesirable outcomes for her love. "Even when he was wearing his football uniform, he looked small," Shirley said years later.

She knew enough about football to understand that Clint was doing well. Even if she had not been able to deduce that on her own, the enthusiastic cheers for him during the games, and the adoration that flowed to him afterward, would have told her so. Typically the couple would attend a party at Clint's fraternity house after a home game. During football season all of the fraternity houses were hubs of activity, and Clint's fraternity, Phi Delta Theta, never failed to celebrate Tech wins in appropriate fashion. Clint normally arrived to find himself the center of attention.

"Clint knew everybody, not really the girls, but all the guys, and they would all want to talk to him about that day's game," Shirley said. "He was extremely popular."

Clint enjoyed Glenn Miller's music; Shirley liked Jeanette Mac-Donald and Nelson Eddy.

Other activities for Tech students and their dates included a juke joint on Piedmont Road called "The Village" that served beer and drew big crowds, particularly when they had Tony Pastor or Will Bradley and his band playing boogie-woogie music.

"We didn't really have to do anything to have fun," Shirley said. "We just had fun together, even if we were just sitting around."

On Sundays the couple would attend a service at Second Ponce De Leon Baptist. Afterward they would stop to get an ice cream cone at a place on Piedmont Road before Clint would take Shirley to the bus station to head back to Milledgeville. Both would then use the remainder of the day to prepare for the week, which meant school for both and football practices for Clint.

And in the week after the Kentucky game, that meant preparing for Alabama.

No team in the country had a better line than the Crimson Tide. All season long, teams had bounced off Alabama's line as if it were made of concrete rather than flesh and bone. Georgia had been able to do nothing against them for three quarters before finally winning a battle of conditioning that allowed them to score three times late in the game. What was shaping up now was a most intriguing pairing of Alabama's muscle against Tech's quickness.

Bobby Dodd surmised that Alabama would not play cautiously as it had against Georgia. After taking a 10 – 0 lead, the Tide had tried to sit on the ball, even quick-kicking to leave the team's fate in the hands of the defense. Dodd knew that wasn't going to happen a second time.

Alabama's defense had allowed just 324 total yards in seven games, which meant opponents were averaging just 46 yards a game. And they had allowed just 27 points, 21 of which had been scored by Georgia in its fourth-quarter comeback win. Dodd's offense-oriented mind told him he needed to work his troops hard to sharpen their passing game. Tech would run some plays into the line to keep Alabama's defense honest, but Tech's best chances of moving the ball against one of the best lines in the country lay in putting the ball in the air and practicing deception.

A sellout crowd of 33,000 was expected, though the exact number could only be guessed, since military personnel could buy tickets for 55 cents to sit in a section reserved for servicemen. Tech's upcoming November 28 game against Georgia had already been declared a sellout.

Bowl talk continued to escalate, with the Rose Bowl's hefty weight carrying most of the conversation. Rose Bowl officials were determined not to let a Southern bowl steal the top matchup for New Year's Day. Anticipating that the winner of the Georgia – Georgia Tech game would finish the season undefeated and at the top of the polls, the Rose Bowl had decided—though no Rose Bowl official would go on record saying so—that whichever team won the battle of Georgia on November 28 would be invited to the Rose Bowl. Such a move would break the precedent of having the Pacific Coast Conference champion select its opponent.

Other speculation continued to suggest that Tech would meet Boston College in the Sugar Bowl even if they finished the season undefeated.

To Dodd's credit, he took an unfamiliar tack following Tech's Wednesday afternoon practice. Instead of downplaying his team to the newspapers, he expressed confidence that Tech could win the game.

"Well, the game with Alabama is waiting for the dice to start rolling," Dodd told reporters. "We realize we will face a team stronger than Notre Dame with probably the best line in the country. But our team is much better than when we played Notre Dame, and I think we have a chance to beat Alabama or any other team.

"One thing I particularly like about our boys this year is this: I think our players have the best mental attitude of any team I ever coached. They have confidence in themselves, but never have underrated any opponent. They have gone into games keyed up, but never jittery."

Alabama coach Frank Thomas suddenly had other things to worry about than the game with Tech after learning that his mother had fallen seriously ill. He rushed to East Chicago, Indiana, to be at her side, and his arrival in Atlanta in time for the game was left in doubt.

Alabama planned to conduct its final practice of the week on Friday afternoon before boarding a streamline train to Atlanta and spending the night at the Georgia Terrace Hotel. Thomas's uncertain status created the possibility of an interesting scenario: If Thomas could not get to Atlanta in time for the game, each of the big-time programs would be guided by assistants, with Paul Burnum calling the shots for Alabama while Dodd was directing Tech.

All of the big radio networks decided to broadcast the Tech – Alabama game over their airwaves, even though Notre Dame would be playing Michigan at the same time. Among them was the Blue Network, the on-air name in 1942 – 46 of the radio production and distribution service that later became the American Broadcasting Company. Harry Wismer was scheduled to be the announcer for the Blue Network and took time to attend a Georgia Tech fish fry the Friday afternoon before the game. Wismer had played college football at Florida and then Michigan State, and in a precursor of what would become the norm in sports broadcasting in future years, he used his time at the fish fry to pick Dodd's brain about some of the nuances of what Tech would be doing on offense. He knew that a basic understanding of the Tech offense would help him convey the action more vividly to his listeners.

"Coach Dodd's help certainly relieves my mind for Saturday," Wismer told *The Atlanta Constitution*. "I'd be scared stiff to try to follow Tech without having any idea of how they're lining up and who is handling the ball in the intricate offensive set-up which varies so much."

On November 13, 1942—Friday the Thirteenth—the day before the Tech – Alabama game, Japanese torpedoes hit the USS *Atlanta* during the Naval Battle of Guadalcanal, and the ship sank off Guadalcanal's Lunga Point. Slightly more than a year had passed since the day when Atlanta swelled with pride at the launching of the ship bearing the city's name. The war felt a little more personal each day to the citizens of Atlanta. Worrying about what might happen could have filled every day with anxiety, which made diversions such as college football even more welcome. Such diversions served as small but helpful reminders of what made freedom worth fighting for.

* * * * *

Colleges usually tried to schedule a weak opponent for homecoming weekend so alumni could watch their team dominate the field. Alabama certainly did not fit that bill as Tech's homecoming opponent on a splendid November Saturday. On the contrary, Alabama was a formidable foe. Bobby Dodd called the Tide "the best team we have seen in two years, or maybe four."

A favorite among the homecoming activities on the Tech campus was the traditional "Ramblin' Wrecks" parade, in which contraptions of all ilk were pieced together to somehow operate like automobiles. Because of the war effort, Tech students opted to push the cars along the parade route to save gas, and all of the contraptions were donated for scrap afterward to help the cause.

Tech donned dark blue jerseys for the game. Dodd had introduced these jerseys during the 1939 Orange Bowl, and the team periodically pulled them out for special occasions such as the Alabama game. Tech's jerseys and Alabama's traditional crimson made

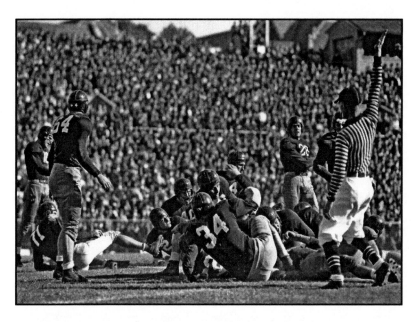

Action during the 1942 Georgia Tech-Alabama clash, which proved to be Tech' finest performance of the season.

brilliant contrasts against the green grass on the Flats of Grant Field. A crowd of 34,000, many of them from nearby military installations, joined representatives from the Sugar and Orange bowls at the game, while radio broadcasted the contest to all corners of the world—except to Coach Aleck's house, per his doctor's orders. Thomas managed to catch a flight to Atlanta in time to join his team for the game, leaving Dodd to match football intellects against Alabama's head coach.

Castleberry ignited a first-quarter drive by fielding a punt on the run, breaking two tackles, and returning the ball 28 yards to the Tech 40. He then opened the offensive series with a 20-yard burst up the middle. On the following play the freshman sensation caught a pass at the Alabama 20 and took the ball to the 9, following which he ran again to the 4. Castleberry then took the snap and dropped back to pass, cocking the ball back as if ready to fire, but instead Ralph Plaster raced past and took the ball off his hand en route to the end zone to score the first running touchdown of the

season against Alabama's stellar line. Tech had once again successfully employed the Statue of Liberty play, as they had in every game
to that point of the season. Eleven minutes into the game, the
touchdown put Tech ahead 7 – 0. For the remainder of the game,
Tech's battered defense turned back one Crimson Tide drive after
another, with Castleberry continuing to stand out during the gallant effort. If he wasn't knocking down passes, he was using his
slight body to drag down larger Alabama running backs. He saved
one touchdown by tackling an Alabama back who had bolted 47
yards, and twice he knocked away touchdown passes. Castleberry's
defense even stood out on offense. When Alabama's All-American
Joe Domnanovich intercepted a pass, Castleberry tackled him at
the Tech 15 to save a touchdown.

Accounts of the game noted that the officials almost lost control of the game through their reluctance to call penalties. They did
manage to blow the whistle when Alabama tackle Don Whitmire
pressed his knee into Castleberry's face, which resulted in a 15-yard
penalty, a warning, and some laughter—even by Castleberry. At the
end of the day, Tech held on for a 7 – 0 win in a game that lasted
just 2 hours 1 minute—including a 16-minute halftime and a slight
delay when officials ordered the removal of a suspicious cast from
an Alabama player's arm.

Thomas told reporters afterward that his team had won many
games, but he had never been more proud of them than for their
play in a game they had lost.

"They lost to a great team—a very great team," Thomas said. "It
will take a lot of ball club to beat that Tech outfit."

Always personable, Dodd teased reporters after the game, saying, "Alex can move over now. I'm ready to share his bed after that
game. I'm tickled to death. Our boys beat, in Alabama, the toughest team we've met. Our backs were great, especially Castleberry
and Plaster, but it was those fine boys in the line who stopped
Alabama's hard-hitting backs."

Wrote Romney Wheeler of the Associated Press, "Alabama
opened its quail season yesterday, 17 days ahead of schedule, and
the first shooting was at Grant Field, Atlanta, before 34,000 game
wardens."

Castleberry's performance so captured Fred Russell of *The*

Nashville Banner that he wrote, "I know of only one way to stop Castleberry, and that's to repeal the freshman eligibility rule."

Dodd, who earned Southeastern Conference Coach of the Week honors for the win, visited Coach Aleck after the game and filled him in on the details. Coach Aleck had spent the afternoon reading William Makepeace Thackeray's *Henry Esmond*. An English novelist and humorist, Thackeray targeted the upper class with his ironic depictions and humor, which amused Coach Aleck no end given his dislike of social elitists. Coach Aleck's wife had attended the game and commented on how news from the game was parceled to her husband.

"Why, it seems that Lilla, the maid, slipped in and told him the score at the half," she said. "But that was all. Until I got home, of course. But I didn't try to tell him about that game. I knew he didn't admire my way of describing a football game. I'd tried it before. So pretty soon Bobby Dodd came along, and—well, he and Alex had a sort of private session. I'm pretty sure that Bobby gave him all of the—what you call the 'low-down' on that game."

Across the state, Georgia won big for the second consecutive week with a convincing 40 – 0 thrashing of Chattanooga. Frankie Sinkwich had moved to fullback and gained a season-high 141 yards in 19 runs, while Charley Trippi gained 136 yards in 12 carries from the same backfield. The performances by both Georgia teams fueled the excitement of the entire state—and nation—for their November 28 matchup. Both teams had already talked to officials from all the bowls. Each team had just one game separating it from what promised to be their historic meeting. Tech would play Florida, while Georgia played Auburn.

In the background, feedback about the positive effects of wartime football remained constant. Wrote *Atlanta Journal* columnist Morgan Blake, "None who observed the poise of 18-year-old Clinton Castleberry in that game with Alabama Saturday can doubt that he and boys his age will be able to hold their own in real warfare with older men. No one need worry about American boys of 18 and 19; they are grown up, and they know what it's all about. Charlie Morgan, now in the Marines, said something following the game Saturday that impressed me.

"In the war Castleberry would be in a more dangerous situation than facing Alabama on a football field, but he won't find any harder, tougher job than battling that Alabama team and snatching victory from them."

In addition to reaching countless military men via the radio with his football heroics, Castleberry's season began to stir Heisman talk.

New York's Downtown Athletic Club (DAC) presented an annual award to the young man selected by voters throughout the country as the "most outstanding player in college football." The inaugural trophy, then known as the "DAC Trophy," had been awarded on December 9, 1935, to Jay Berwanger of the University of Chicago. In advance of the occasion, the Downtown Athletic Club had commissioned New York sculptor Frank Eilscu to create a bronze statue of a football player for the trophy, and Eliscu called upon his friend Ed Smith, who played for the New York University football team, to be his model. Eliscu's bronze depicted a football player avoiding one tackler with a crossover step while giving another a stiff arm. The finished statue weighed 45 pounds and stood 14 inches long, 13½ inches high, and 6½ inches wide.

At the time of the inaugural award, John Heisman, the famed coaching genius who could count Coach Aleck as one of his most accomplished understudies, worked as the Downtown Athletic Club's director of athletics. Heisman died October 3, 1936, and to honor one of college football's all-time greatest coaches and the man club members had come to know, the DAC Trophy became the "The Heisman Memorial Trophy Award."

The award didn't have the glamour in its first years that it would attain years later, but it gained prestige every season. There had been seven Heisman winners by 1942, and each had been a senior. That a freshman's name was even in the mix spoke to the kind of excitement Castleberry had created during his first season of college football. Georgia Tech's Jackrabbit had sportswriters around the country talking about the possibility of Castleberry winning the award. Also in the running were Sinkwich and Columbia's Paul Governali, who were both seniors. Governali, who played quarterback, led the nation in passing.

Castleberry's case was helped by his strong performances in big markets like Chicago—when Tech played Notre Dame in nearby

South Bend, Indiana—and Washington D.C.—just 50 miles down the road from where Tech played Navy. A strong finish by Castleberry and an undefeated season for Georgia Tech just might earn him the coveted Heisman. If so, he would be the first player from a school where Heisman had coached to win the award.

Two days after Tech defeated Alabama, word arrived from California that the U.S. Army had granted approval to the Rose Bowl organization to again hold the bowl in Pasadena. Almost immediately after Colonel H. E. Beal informed the Rose Bowl Committee of the army's decision, the talk turned to how much the most prestigious of all bowl games wanted Sinkwich and Georgia to take on the Pacific Coast Conference champion.

While Georgia ranked first on the committee's wish list, Tech, Boston College, and Tulsa likewise remained among the undefeated and untied teams eligible for the game.

17

One More Before Georgia

Before a battle of Georgia's unbeaten teams could take place on November 28, Tech would have to beat Florida and Georgia would have to get past Auburn. Most considered the latter to be a foregone conclusion.

Tech had outscored opposing teams 192 to 32, while Georgia had outscored its opponents by a margin of 320 to 49.

One writer compared the torn state of Georgia with its two undefeated football teams to Kentucky's divided loyalties during the Civil War. "In the bluegrass brothers parted, the one to don the blue of the North, the other the gray of the South," he wrote, "[while] mother wiped her eyes on her apron and remained loyal to her sons."

Georgia remained the top-ranked team in the country, followed by Tech in the second spot and Boston College in third. Many expressed displeasure with the ranking system. Midwest and Big Ten teams in particular questioned the strength of the top three teams' schedules. Grantland Rice wrote, "It must be admitted, in the way of fairness, that the leading Midwestern teams play a far harder schedule than many of today's nominees have had to face."

Of the country's three leading teams, Rice believed that Tech had played the toughest schedule to date, followed by Georgia and Boston College.

United Press International named Bobby Dodd the National Coach of the Week after Tech's win over Alabama. Accolades aside, however, Tech paid a heavy price in beating the Crimson Tide. Once again the squad came up limping afterward, prompting Dodd to cancel Monday's practice prior to the Florida game. None of the regulars even scrimmaged until Thursday's practice.

Coach Aleck left his bed to return to the Tech campus that same Thursday and spent two hours working in his office. His doctor granted him two hours a day at the office but drew the line at attending games, leaving Coach Aleck to consider which classic to read on Saturday afternoon—well out of radio range—as Tech's season continued to unfold.

Though the Gators had won just three of nine games on the season, they were viewed as a dangerous team now that their entire squad was healthy. Florida's good health and Tech's injuries added up to a possible upset. Tom Lieb had become the Gators' head coach in 1940 and had beaten Tech in both their meetings since then, which added to the upset talk. In years past a healthy contingent of Gators fans had made the trip to Atlanta, but this year Tech expected a sparse showing from the visitors due to transportation problems and the Gators' lackluster season to date.

Even after a less-than-grueling week of practice for his beat-up squad, Dodd elected to start his second string against the Gators, a strategy that lasted until the Gators drove to a first down at the Tech 11. Dodd then rushed in the first string before the first quarter had concluded. Two Castleberry passes helped Tech's first scoring drive stay alive to give Tech a 7 – 0 lead early in the second quarter. Tech then intercepted a pass on Florida's ensuing drive, but they fumbled a lateral that allowed the Gators to recover the ball at the Tech 27. Given a reprieve, the Gators quickly scored a touchdown to tie the score at 7 – 7 heading into the intermission.

Castleberry ignited the lackluster Tech squad in the second half. Midway through the third quarter, he returned a punt 26 yards to the Florida 45. After a gain of 5 yards on first down, Castleberry dropped back as if to pass, and just when he cocked his arm, Davey Eldredge zipped behind him, grabbing the ball from Castleberry's hand. Eldredge then scooted 40 yards for a touchdown, producing yet another successful Statue of Liberty play.

Castleberry added a 2-yard touchdown run in the fourth quarter, squirting through the Gator line to put Tech up 20 – 7, which would be the final score of Tech's ninth consecutive win. Late in the game, however, Castleberry suffered a knee injury that left him questionable for the Georgia game.

Castleberry probably damaged the cartilage in his knee, though not to the extent that he couldn't move. Knee injuries in 1942 were far more devastating than they would be in the future, simply because the surgical procedures employed to repair them were so primitive then. Fortunately for Tech, the team doctors did not feel that Castleberry's injury warranted surgery.

Castleberry's injury aside, Dodd left Grant Field with a positive attitude—at least outwardly. "With one eye on Georgia next Saturday and with our boys well battered from the bruising Alabama game last Saturday, we had no idea we could rout Florida," Dodd said. "We were tickled to win at all, especially since Florida really played the fine game they did."

* * * * *

Georgia had defeated the same Florida team by a score of 75 – 0 two weeks earlier. Relative scores against common opponents can be misleading, however. Anything can happen—that's why the games are played. Consider, for example, what took place in Columbus, Georgia, on Saturday, November 21.

While the Yellow Jackets were facing Florida, the Georgia Bulldogs squared off against Auburn at Memorial Stadium. Auburn had lost to both Tech and Florida, and Georgia had defeated Auburn a year earlier when Frankie Sinkwich threw a late touchdown pass to break a scoreless tie. With a crowd of 20,000 watching, the Bulldogs appeared to pick up where they had left off, winning the coin toss and marching to a touchdown in the first four minutes for a 6 – 0 lead.

Based on the outcomes of previous games, that start signaled the beginning of the end for Auburn, except that it didn't happen that way. Auburn dug deep for an inner resolve and answered the number 1 Bulldogs with two touchdowns of their own.

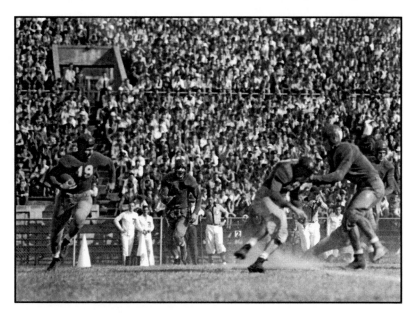

Clint Castleberry shown in action for Georgia Tech against Florida in their 1942 clash at Grant Field. Castleberry suffered a knee injury in the game that would haunt him the remainder of the season.

By halftime, Auburn led 14 – 6.

After a scoreless third quarter, Auburn scored another touchdown that Georgia matched before Auburn's line swarmed Sinkwich in his own end zone to force a fumble. Auburn fell on the football for a touchdown, and the 27 – 13 upset was complete, snapping Georgia's winning streak at 15 games.

Auburn coach Jack Meagher had coached a brilliant game against Georgia, employing his substitute players to help keep a fresh team on the field for four quarters. For Meagher, the win was particularly sweet. He would coach the Tigers the following week against Clemson, then return to active duty in the U.S. Marine Corps. Eleven of his Tiger players were slated to join their coach in military service. Defeating the top team in the country created a nice memory to take overseas.

Auburn's upset appeared to kill the Bulldogs' hopes of playing in the Rose Bowl on New Year's Day, and the dream of having two unbeaten Georgia teams meet for all the marbles also died in Columbus. Boston College jumped Tech to claim the top spot in the polls, while Tech remained at number 2 and Georgia dropped to number 6.

Castleberry had proven beyond any doubt that despite his size, he had the skills to play major college football and even dominate a game. Nor could the Jackrabbit's heart be questioned; his five-foot-nine, 160-pound frame was all heart. Yet the cumulative effects of playing at his size could not be discounted. There had been the shoulder injury, and now his knee was dinged up. Georgia had a physical and talented team. Did Castleberry have enough heart in his beat-up body to lead Tech to one more victory?

18

The Much-Awaited Showdown

Georgia and Georgia Tech first met on a football field in 1893, and by 1942 the two teams had played 35 times. Georgia had taken 18 wins to Tech's 12 in the series, and there had been five ties.

A palpable animosity continued to exist between the two schools. Georgia had a well-rounded liberal arts curriculum, while Tech offered an engineering/technical education. Tech graduates and students long had looked down on their Georgia counterparts, maintaining that they lacked the intelligence of a Tech student, while Georgia students perceived Tech students as social misfits with slide rulers. Friends, family members, even brothers could find themselves on opposite sides of the fence.

M.H. Furchgott and his brother, Charlie, attended Boys' High together, even though, as mentioned earlier, Charlie had remained at Boys' High considerably longer thanks to the eligibility rule. Upon graduating, M.H. went to Tech and Charlie to Georgia, where both played football. M.H. spoke of the disparity in the demands on football players at Tech and Georgia, as well as the demands placed on players from other schools Tech played on a regular basis.

"We played about five teams [at Tech] that demanded that all the players go to class every day," M.H. said. "We played Notre Dame, Navy, Duke, North Carolina, and Tulane. Of the teams in the SEC at the time, only Georgia Tech, Vanderbilt, and Tulane really demanded that their football players go to classes and maintain passing grades.

"My brother was a phys-ed major at Georgia. My sophomore year I was taking calculus, physics, mechanical drawing, English literature, and a civil engineering course. At the same time my brother was taking music appreciation and a coaching course, and the toughest course he had was history."

Such feelings, even among brothers, only served to fan the flames of the bitter rivalry. The teams simply did not like one another.

"Actually, we didn't like any of them," Bob Sheldon said. "But they were real good ballplayers. Excellent players. Butts we despised. But he was a damn good coach."

In a whimsical exercise, *The Atlanta Journal* compiled a chart of Tech and Georgia's comparative scores against common opponents, then predicted the result of their head-to-head matchup based on each comparison. The results looked like this:

(1) Based on their results against Kentucky, Tech would beat Georgia 39 – 0.
(2) Based on their games against Chattanooga, Georgia would win 22 – 0.
(3) Based on the Alabama games, Georgia would win 4 – 0.
(4) Based on Florida, Georgia would win 62 – 0.
(5) Based on Auburn, Tech would win 29 – 0.

The paper went on to point out how silly comparative scores were by noting that if the Georgia – Auburn game had followed the script of both teams' games against Florida, Georgia would have beaten Auburn 81 – 0.

In other words, comparative scores meant nothing. Football teams were different animals at different stages of a season—different in health, chemistry, state of mind, experience, and preparation.

In a historical context, Tech's fortunes looked bleak heading into the Georgia game even though the Yellow Jackets were undefeated and carried a higher ranking. Tech had never won at Georgia's Sanford Stadium, where the game would be played, and none of Tech's twelve senior players had been a part of a victory against Georgia.

Coach Aleck harbored a bad premonition about the game. Based on the circumstances and health of his team, he couldn't help feeling that Georgia would throttle Tech in Athens, and he said as much to a friend the week of the game. He figured that Dodd had put forth a superior coaching effort in motivating and guiding the team to an unheard-of three peaks in the same season. The first peak had been climbed against Notre Dame in early October; the second was reached against Navy later in the month, a momentum they had managed to nurse through the Duke game. Finally, they had climbed their third and highest peak against Alabama in November. Most teams were happy to reach one peak in a season. That a team like Tech—lacking the depth and physical tools of many of its opponents—should reach a fourth peak seemed too much to hope. In Coach Aleck's mind, Tech had overachieved to reach 9 – 0, and the toll was a physically spent and mentally exhausted team.

Georgia had a bigger, more physical team with more weapons than Tech, including Frankie Sinkwich, Charley Trippi, and George Poschner. Tech's line play had been stellar all season, but now they were beaten up. And so was Castleberry, the team's best player.

Having lost to Auburn the week before, Georgia had one game in which to salvage their season, and Butts didn't hesitate to remind them of that fact. He drilled, prepped, motivated, and whipped up his team through a tough week of practice leading into the Tech game.

"Since we lost to Auburn the week before, Coach Butts was not in a good mood," Trippi said. "I'll tell you, you wouldn't have wanted to be at practice that week. It was hard and vicious. He really got us ready to play a tough game.

"We weren't in a good frame of mind. I think the most difficult thing you'll ever do in football is to play against somebody that got beat the week before. We came out like tigers for the Georgia Tech game. Unfortunately for Georgia Tech, they were our opponents that weekend. Coach Butts really got us ready to play."

Tech's belief that they were a team of destiny might have been the biggest plus they had going for them. They had beaten Notre Dame in South Bend, something they had never done before. They had beaten Navy for the first time, they had won at Duke for the first time, they had beaten a Fred Lieb – coached Florida team for the first time, and they had beaten a Crimson Tide team that was said to have the best line in the nation. With all those firsts behind them, a win at Sanford Stadium looked more than possible; it looked almost predestined—unless you were Coach Aleck or Bobby Dodd, who recognized that his finely tuned machine was running on fumes.

Hoping to pull one last rabbit out of the hat, Dodd conducted closed practices the week of the Georgia game, emphasizing pass defense in the hope of slowing down the enormous firepower of the Bulldogs' passing game. Sinkwich had thrown three touchdowns in Georgia's 21 – 0 victory over Tech in 1941, and two of the receivers who had caught those touchdowns, Poschner and Lamar "Race Horse" Davis, still wore Georgia uniforms. The Bulldogs' passing attack had become even more refined and dangerous in 1942. After ten games they had completed 110 passes in 220 attempts for 1,951 yards—huge numbers for 1942. Sinkwich and Trippi had thrown the bulk of those passes.

Closed practices also allowed Dodd to conceal the extent of Castleberry's injury and the true degree to which his team was beaten up. Dodd did not even know whether Castleberry could play, much less whether he could be effective.

Castleberry continued to receive accolades for the way he had played during Tech's 9 – 0 run. Grantland Rice called him "one of the best ball carriers of the year—possibly the best." Speculation about who would win the Heisman Trophy paled in comparison to talk about who would make All-America, which carried top billing. While Castleberry's chances for the Heisman were real and subject to continued debate in newspapers across the country, the idea of a freshman making an All-America team struck a hot button. Most felt he had played well enough to earn consideration for the top awards in college football, but some argued that such awards should be saved for upperclassmen, and a freshman should have to pay his dues. The obvious counterpoint to such logic was that the country was at war, and any player, freshman or not, could find himself the following year in a different sort of uniform, fighting and perhaps dying for his country. Any game, any season, could be that player's last. In such circumstances, how could a young man be denied just consideration merely because he was not yet an upperclassman?

The nation's sporting attention turned to the state of Georgia that week of November 1942, as football fans and pundits tried to forecast which team would win the November 28 contest and who was the better player, Castleberry or Sinkwich. Comparisons between the two ran daily in the papers. While Sinkwich had more total yards of offense with 1,995, Castleberry averaged 8.5 yards per carry. Sinkwich was considered the better passer, having completed 76 passes for 1,300 yards. Tech did not keep passing records, but many of Castleberry's completions had produced grand results, and his punt-returning ability and defense were second to none. Even *The New York Times* got caught up in the hype; two days before the game, the esteemed newspaper featured a comparison between Castleberry and Sinkwich with side-by-side photos of the pair under a headline that read, "Georgia Peaches: They Will Pass – You Take Your Choice."

❊ ❊ ❊ ❊ ❊

There had been no official word that Edwin Atherton, Pacific Coast Conference athletic commissioner, had been granted authority to begin negotiating an opponent for the Pacific Coast Conference champion to meet in the Rose Bowl. Behind the scenes, however, another story began to evolve in the week before the Tech – Georgia game. Overtures from those controlling the Rose Bowl suggested that if Tech were to beat Georgia, they would be invited to the game. Such an invitation meant a great deal to the coffers of any school, guaranteeing a minimum payout of $100,000, enough to go a long way in 1942. And similar overtures were made to Georgia. "People from the Rose Bowl came to town the week of the Georgia Tech game," Trippi said. "And they declared that the winner of the game would go to the Rose Bowl."

So a victory for either school was likely to mean more than just a rivalry win—it meant a trip to the most prestigious bowl game and cash.

Some commentators, not knowing of the Rose Bowl overtures, speculated that Tech would go to the Sugar Bowl even if they won the Georgia game, so that they could play a higher-ranked opponent than they would face in the Rose Bowl. The Pacific Coast Conference champion would have at least one loss, since the contenders—Washington State, Southern California, and UCLA—had all lost a game. That boded well for Georgia's Rose Bowl chances, as did the fact that people in California still liked the idea of having Georgia play in Pasadena on New Year's Day; simply put, they deemed Sinkwich and the Bulldogs a sexier possibility than Castleberry and Tech.

Speculation aside, both teams knew what a win might mean. Between the rough practices administered by Butts and the promise of a Rose Bowl berth, Georgia had plenty of incentive to rebound from its loss to Auburn.

"The Rose Bowl was one game you wanted to play in," Trippi said. "There was nothing more glamorous than going to the Rose Bowl. We knew that playing in that game would be quite an honor."

On top of that, a trip to the Rose Bowl would place the Bulldogs in their second consecutive bowl game. They had never participated in a bowl game before their 40 – 26 win over Texas Christian University in the Orange Bowl on New Year's Day, 1942.

War news remained constant on newspaper front pages. The Soviet Union provided big news in the week before the Tech – Georgia game, beginning a counteroffensive at Stalingrad and killing 15,000 Nazis. More personal war stories circulated daily as well, permeating the lives of young football players and all Americans.

On Tuesday night before the Georgia game, Tech's team was honored at Atlanta's Capital City Club, where, according to O.B. Keeler's account in *The Atlanta Journal*, they were served "roast beef such as this correspondent has not encountered in more than a dozen years." At the conclusion of the banquet, Chip Robert, the master of ceremonies, awarded Tech team captain Jack Marshall a portrait of Bobby Beers, their fallen teammate. The sobering moment was another reminder, if any was needed, of what awaited most of them when the season finished and their military service began.

Tech went through a light practice on Friday, and Dodd continued to hold his cards close to his vest about the health of Castleberry and his team. He told reporters that Tech trainers were treating wingback Pat McHugh, who had come up lame in practice. Otherwise, according to Tech's interim coach, the Yellow Jackets were in better health than at any other point of the season. Anyone accustomed to Dodd's habitual pregame poor-mouthing—in other words, everyone—could reasonably interpret his remarks as a banner written across the sky that his team was hurting. When asked specifically how Castleberry might do against Georgia, the poker-faced Dodd stayed in character, offering a bluff: "Clint goes best when the game is toughest."

Atlanta hotels began to fill with alumni from both schools, wanting a visit to the big city before making their way to Athens on Saturday for the annual rivalry game. Rooms were booked in advance to facilitate parties after the game, either to revel in victory or drown sorrows. In Athens, school officials worked hard to prepare for the game. Since 42,000 tickets had already been sold, wooden bleachers were added to Sanford Stadium to accommodate more fans. The playing surface had been bald and rough just weeks earlier, but workers had planted winter grass to give the field a green glow. Great efforts were made to procure the best possible officiating crew, and the payoff was landing three of the officials who had successfully worked the Tech – Florida game. Newspapers lauded the trio for aggressively calling the "piling-on" penalty in their efforts to curb what was recognized as one of the most dangerous of infractions.

Fearing major traffic problems on the roads between Atlanta and Athens, Butts lined up extra traffic officers and military personnel to direct traffic, then went public to reassure fans, many of whom had been saving rationed gas for weeks in anticipation of attending the game. There would also be a number of people arriving the old-fashioned way—by horse and carriage.

Fraternity houses on the Georgia campus hung up less-than-flattering signs about Tech—the more insulting the sign, the better. A newspaper photo of Georgia's Sigma Nu house showed the brothers atop their own ramblin' wreck, which was well beaten and turned upside down on their front lawn. Tech students sneaked into Athens during the week and left swaths of yellow paint prominently positioned all over the campus.

Added fervor and animosity was directed toward football writers leading up to the game—those who maintained neutrality as well as those who picked a side. As Jack Troy pointed out in *The Atlanta Constitution*, writers had been "called gutless for refusing to take a stand." He went on to point out that such a stand was hard when the teams appeared so evenly matched. All of the big Eastern newspapers sent at least one representative to Athens to cover the game— no mean feat given the prevailing wartime travel restrictions. Most of the country would be able to hear the game via the Mutual Network, which reached 199 stations. At halftime of the Penn – Cornell game on Thanksgiving Day—two days before the big game—Harry Wismer of the Blue Network hyped the Tech – Georgia game for five minutes. Here is a portion of Wismer's message:

> *Athens, Georgia is the football capital of the world [Saturday]. For it is well understood that there is no opposition for the Rose Bowl. Boston College is no rival. The Rose Bowl will not invite Boston College. The ivy-clad saucer in far-away California wants Tech or Georgia.*
>
> *The South's Sugar and Orange Bowls, well represented here, have been keenly interested in the two teams for weeks. They are not being outdone by the Rose Bowl, whose main attraction is that distance lends enchantment.*

Tech traveled by train from Atlanta to Athens early Saturday morning. After reaching their destination, the team ate lunch at one of the naval dining halls located on the Georgia campus.

The 70-mile stretch of road between Athens and Atlanta swelled with thin-tired autos traveling the wartime speed limit of 35 miles per hour—a limit that was strictly enforced. The scene was reminiscent of the profligate gusto of the salad days before the war. Many of those travelers were anticipating a Tech win and drove along while singing in unison, "California, Here I Come."

The crowded stands in Athens for the 1942 showdown between Georgia Tech and Georgia. Note all the military personnel in attendance.

A bracing autumn day greeted a crowd estimated to number from 42,000 to 50,000 for the 3 P.M. kickoff in Sanford Stadium.

"They brought in temporary stands," Trippi said. "I think the capacity crowd at that game came to about 50,000, which was one of the big games of the year. Normally we'd play to maybe 40,000, but with the extra seats they increased the attendance to 50,000. You couldn't have squeezed another person into that stadium. Oh, it was a beautiful day to play. We wore the red jerseys. Every home game we would wear red. I think we wore our black jerseys one game, but we never did that against Georgia Tech."

* * * * *

Sinkwich won the coin toss at midfield, and Georgia received the opening kickoff. Poschner took the kick at the 20 and returned it 16 yards before fumbling.

Tech recovered.

The team of destiny appeared to be off and running to the start they needed to pull off one last unexpected win. Castleberry added to the momentum on the first play by darting around left end for 5 yards. Sanford Stadium began to vibrate from the crowd noise. Fans from both schools stood on their feet, sensing something special on the next play. A first down would establish a much-needed early rhythm. Georgia needed a stop to quiet Tech's confidence and the crowd, and that's exactly what the Bulldog defense managed to accomplish on the next play, causing Ralph Plaster to fumble. Though Plaster recovered his own fumble, Tech got penalized 15 yards from the spot of the foul for holding on the play. Then a series of miscues forced Tech to punt, quieting the Tech cheering section.

Both teams appeared tight and nervous, which was hardly surprising given the stakes and the hype leading up to the game. One mistake followed another in the early going, with neither team able to take advantage. Late in the first quarter, however, Sinkwich intercepted a Castleberry pass and returned the ball 8 yards to the Tech 36. Sinkwich then ambled 17 yards off tackle before Castleberry tackled him. Trippi tacked on another yard around end, then took the snap on the third play of the drive looking as if he would run. When Tech's defense bought the fake and their backs moved in, Trippi stopped and drew back his arm while looking at the "Race Horse," who had found a clearing at the 15. Trippi's perfectly arched pass hit Lamar Davis in stride at the 9, and Davis darted into the end zone to put Georgia up 7 – 0 nine minutes into the game.

The first period ended with Georgia driving again at the Tech 24, and to Tech's dismay, the change of quarters did nothing to thwart the Georgia drive. Poschner hauled in a Sinkwich pass and advanced 18 yards to the Tech 6, and from there the "Race Horse" once again found the end zone, scoring on an end-around to put the Bulldogs up 14 – 0.

Sinkwich and Trippi ran the ball as well as any backs in the country, yet Georgia's passing game continued to be the biggest problem for Tech's zone defense. Butts's build had earned him the nickname of "Mister Five by Five"—a moniker that didn't exactly evoke images of grace. Yet his immense knowledge of the passing game allowed Georgia receivers to maneuver through opposing defenses with confident precision. Butts didn't spread his players all over the field; rather, they did a lot of crossing action in the back-field, faking to the fullback to set up passing routes that were designed to find the seams of a zone defense.

"They ran some beautiful patterns, and Sinkwich and Trippi were both good passers," Sheldon said.

Georgia continued to execute their pinpoint passing game toward the end of the second quarter, marching straight up the field on another drive to the Tech 4. Then a personal foul penalty moved the ball back 15 yards, and Tech fans hoped that was the harbinger for a change in momentum. On the next play Sinkwich tried to force a pass into the middle of the Tech defense, and Castleberry stepped in to make the interception in the end zone for a touchback to give Tech the ball at the 20.

Several plays later, with Tech facing a fourth down at their own 30, punter Jim Luck faked the kick then passed to Castleberry, who took the ball to the Tech 46. Georgia had dominated the half but led only 14 – 0. If Tech could manage a touchdown before the half, they would be right back in the game. The Tech cheering section came to life, and Castleberry seemed to gain energy from the momentum shift and completed a pass on the next play, taking Tech to the Georgia 41.

Accounts differ about what happened next. What is known is that Castleberry swept around end and got tackled, and after all the other players had gotten up, the Jackrabbit remained on the ground. The knee he'd injured in the Florida game had given out. Trainers helped him to the sideline, then escorted him to the locker room.

Shirley Poole knew her boyfriend's knee had bothered him a great deal after the Florida game. She had remained at home with her parents over the post-Thanksgiving weekend, and was listening to the game on the radio among her relatives.

"Wouldn't you know, all of my relatives, aunts and uncles, went to the University of Georgia," said Poole with a chuckle.

Sixty-seven years after the game, Poole still carries a vivid memory of what happened. "I can still remember hearing that he had hurt his knee, and that made me ill," she said.

The question still debated is whether Castleberry's knee gave out on its own, or whether Poschner did the job.

M.H. Furchgott, who was a freshman and did not play for the

Tech varsity at the time, attended the game and reported what he saw happen when Castleberry went down.

"Clint was tackled, and when they were on the ground, Poschner twisted his foot," Furchgott said. "Poschner didn't get called for a penalty. The play was over and nobody noticed it, at least none of the officials did."

Trippi made no mention of Poschner twisting Castleberry's ankle.

"We knew Castleberry was a tough ballplayer. He'd had a great year," Trippi said. "But he got hurt early in the game against us. Of course, when you're hurt, you can't play. I didn't get to see much of him in that ballgame."

Sheldon didn't see Poschner twist Castleberry's knee, but he "wouldn't put it past" the young player he remembered. "He was mostly mouth and a damn good ballplayer, I guess," Sheldon said years later. "But not the cleanest."

John Crawford was in uniform for Tech that day and didn't remember a dirty play. "A Georgia player tackled Castleberry, who got injured on the play. It put him out for the rest of the game," Crawford said. "And he was the spark plug. If we didn't have him on that team, we didn't have the greatest team in the world. Losing him, that was demoralizing."

Crawford paused, then added, "Georgia was a very good team, too."

Disheartened when Castleberry left the game, Tech lost momentum, and their drive stalled. They punted out of bounds at the Georgia 13. On the next play, Trippi received the snap.

"I was supposed to roll out and throw a pass in the flats," Trippi said. "And when I rolled out I saw a lot of daylight and just ran up the field and picked up my blockers."

By the time Trippi stopped running, he had covered 87 yards and scored a backbreaking touchdown that put Georgia up 20 – 0 at the half. Castleberry listened to Trippi's run on the radio in the Tech dressing room.

During the intermission, Dodd learned that Castleberry would not be returning to the game; he could barely walk. The somber mood in the Georgia Tech dressing room reflected a team and a coach who suddenly realized their bubble had burst. Dodd, who normally had the answer to everything, had little to say at the half. Crawford felt that Dodd's inexperience as a head coach showed at this point, and that not having Coach Aleck hurt the team.

"It didn't do us any good at all, because Dodd had not had any experience as the head coach," Crawford said. "Because when we got behind, normally we'd go in and they'd get on the chalkboard and draw what was wrong and what we should do and this, that, and the other. At the half at Georgia, when we were behind 20 – 0, there was no chalkboard talk or anything else. We were behind 20 – 0 and there was, apparently, nothing we could do."

"Jack Marshall, a good friend of mine, and captain of the team, felt like he should have gotten up and said something," Sheldon said. "Because Dodd said we were doing as well as he expected, and Marshall wanted him to stir us up. That was typical of Dodd. He wasn't a rah-rah guy. He was a fundamentalist."

Had Castleberry been able to play in the second half, there might at least have been a flicker of hope that some magic might happen.

"He had a physical impact on the team when he came in," said Sheldon of Castleberry. "He would lift us up. When he came in, it was like, 'we're going to get going now.' We had great confidence with him in the game."

But even if the Jackrabbit had been ready for duty in the second half, Tech's fate appeared sealed.

"No doubt, losing Castleberry hurt their offense—their defense, too, he was quite a player on defense," Trippi said. "But the way we were ready to play that day, I don't think it would have made much difference. We still would have won it like we did. We were ready to really play a tough ballgame, and we did."

Georgia added two more touchdowns in the second half, and when the final gun sounded they had stormed to a 34 – 0 win.

"We had a great team, but that particular game we just didn't come through," Crawford said.

According to Trippi, Georgia Tech had run into the worst kind of opponent on the last Saturday of November in 1942.

"We opened up the gates on Georgia Tech that day," Trippi said. "Nobody expected us to beat them that badly. And the thing I remember the most is that we won. That's the most memorable thing. Any football game is always tough. And we came out ready to play that ballgame. You never want to play a team that lost the week before, because you're in trouble if you're playing that team."

Sinkwich received most of the credit for Georgia that season, but Trippi made the biggest impression on Sheldon.

"I remember when I caught a cold from the breeze of Trippi running past me one time," said Sheldon with a chuckle.

Coach Aleck opted to go for a drive without a radio the afternoon of the game. When he returned home close to sunset, he learned that Tech had received a 34 – 0 drubbing, the worst defeat in the rivalry's history and the first of Castleberry's football career. The Jackrabbit's heart couldn't overcome his injury or the ferocious Bulldogs.

Dodd spoke graciously in defeat, calling the Bulldogs "the greatest team in the country today."

Ralph McGill wrote:

"Thinking back over the game, I know there is one sight I will not forget. It was not a play in the game, but the sight of the Tech players leaving the field. They were a better team than they showed. They knew it. They could not explain why, for them, their one slack day had to be the biggest day of all.

"And the old Athens bell had a solemn sound to it this Saturday evening. (It rang for roses, it rang for Sinkwich.) It was saying play was done and that the young men of the teams who had played that day were being called. Within a few months, most of them will be in uniform, Georgia and Tech, fighting side by side in the bigger game. The bowl games are a remaining interlude."

In taking the win, Georgia became the lone survivor of the round-robin of Dixie and, accordingly, received its invitation to the Rose Bowl. Sinkwich and the rest of the team grabbed Butts and ushered him fully clothed into the showers, where they soaked him head to toe. Any other time, steam would have risen off the hard-assed coach, but his team had just executed their chief rival in grand style, and he reacted with tears and a smile instead.

Custom dictated that the Georgia players meet after the game to discuss which bowl invitation they wanted to accept. They told the media they would not divulge their choice until 11 P.M. Few doubted their choice would be the Rose Bowl.

"We were all elated after the outcome of the game," Trippi said. "But there was no real celebration. We accepted it like any other game we'd won during the season. Of course, going to the Rose Bowl, we were excited."

Tech's players were not to be afforded the luxury of picking and choosing. In one fell swoop, the team's stock had plummeted like Wall Street during the Great Crash. If the 34 – 0 loss hadn't made them unattractive enough, the fact that their best player had been injured and might not be available for a bowl game transformed Tech into ugly ducklings.

Tom Harmon attended the game. The former All-American running back for the University of Michigan was a lieutenant in the army air corps at the time, stationed at nearby Greenville, South Carolina. Harmon had a BigTen pedigree, but he left impressed with what he had seen.

"What I like best about this Georgia team is the perfect protection they give their passers," Harmon told *The Atlanta Constitution*. "They're safer than money in war bonds."

Harmon had won the Heisman Memorial Trophy in 1940, so his attendance at the game could have been seen as a precursor for the post-game news delivered from New York. Chairman Bill Prince of the Heisman Memorial Trophy Committee made the announcement on behalf of New York's Downtown Athletic Club that Sinkwich had won the Heisman for 1942. Sinkwich went to New York the following week for the ceremony, accompanied by Butts. He wore a U.S. Marine Corps dress uniform to accept the award, though he had not yet been called up for active duty. Due to wartime restrictions on metal use, Sinkwich received a certificate rather than the bronze trophy.

The national and regional voting of sportswriters and broadcasters awarded Sinkwich 1,059 votes, and he led all five of the voting regions in votes. Paul Governali finished second in the voting, followed by Castleberry in third.

Heroes could be made or broken in the sports pages or via the magic of radio. Clint Castleberry had attained a mystical quality, beginning with the days when he had starred for Boys' High in games that could be heard on the radio, and then as the "Jackrabbit" during national broadcasts of Tech games. Week by week,

Castleberry had served his adoring following well by showing how someone could overcome a lack of size to dominate a football game. The colorful descriptions of his winding, evasive touchdown runs and defensive plays only served to romanticize Castleberry even more. So there were more than a few broken hearts when the indestructible hero finally proved human.

Pepper Rodgers could be counted among the disappointed. Rather than sulk about the failure of his hero to produce yet another exciting victory, Rodgers thought about Castleberry's feelings after such a lopsided loss. Never lacking confidence, he decided to console Castleberry. On the Monday after the Georgia game, Rodgers went to the phone book, looked up Castleberry's home number, then picked up the telephone.

"I called him at home, and he was in," Rodgers said. "I told him, 'I'm sorry you lost that game.' He was so nice to me on the telephone. That was wonderful for me. Of course he was only 19. I thought he was Superman. He was my hero. . . Ty Cobb, Jeb Stuart, Clint Castleberry—only heroes I ever had."

Though derailed, Tech's season had not yet reached its conclusion.

Coach Aleck began receiving phone calls from Austin, Texas, at halftime of the Tech-Georgia game. He had not been home to take the calls, because he'd been out on a drive. The caller was Dana Xenophon Bible, head football coach at the University of Texas.

Bible's coaching roots went nearly as deep as Coach Aleck's. He had broken into coaching in 1912 at Mississippi College and remained there through 1915, when he moved to LSU. He had then moved to Texas A&M, remaining there until 1928 before moving to Nebraska. He began coaching at Texas in 1937. Bible had won many conference championships and had the respect of his peers in the coaching profession, including Coach Aleck, who served with Bible on the college football rules committee. Alexander considered the Longhorn coach a friend, but Bible's call to Coach Aleck was not a social call. Texas would be playing in a bowl game for the first time, and as champion of the Southwest Conference the Longhorns had earned the right to invite a worthy opponent to the game. Bible invited Tech to be that opponent in the Cotton Bowl on New Year's Day. Typical of Coach Aleck's gruff and to-the-point manner, he asked his old friend if he had heard the final score of the Tech-Georgia game—which, he reminded Bible, was the worst beating administered by Georgia to Tech in forty years. Bible acknowledged that he had seen the score but dismissed the outcome, noting that Texas had wanted to put together a game against Tech for years.

"Our people out here want to see Georgia Tech and I want to play you," Bible said. "The Cotton Bowl will be filled."

19

Honors and the Cotton Bowl

C lint Castleberry remained on crutches for several days after the Georgia game, nursing his injured knee. Tech had lost its biggest game in years, yet solace could be taken from the belief that Castleberry would someday return from military service to build on what he'd started his freshman season.

Joe Daniel, who played on Tech's freshman team in 1942, happened to be eating breakfast one morning at a little hole-in-the-wall in downtown Atlanta when he ran into Castleberry at the intersection of North Avenue and Spring Street. He knew Castleberry well, since both were freshmen, had many of the same classes, and were on the football team. The two had become friends.

"That just happened to be the morning when the paper came out announcing that he had become an All-American as a freshman," Daniel said. "I happened to be with him when he read the paper, and all he said was, 'I can't believe that.' He was just an average guy and as nice a gentleman as you can imagine. No idea of being what he was. He was just a regular fellow. He was just unusually kind and thoughtful and you couldn't describe a nicer fellow."

Castleberry's magic earned him all-SEC honors and second or third team honors on the various All-American teams. His popularity was such that the jersey he had worn in the Georgia game was auctioned off for $20,000 worth of war bonds at the "Bonds for Victory Ball" in Atlanta on December 7, a year after the Japanese had bombed Pearl Harbor. Frankie Sinkwich's jersey yielded just $3,000 in bonds at the same benefit.

The New York World-Telegram named Coach Aleck football coach of the year as a result of its annual poll of head coaches of the nation's colleges and universities. *The Nashville Banner* selected Wally Butts as the Southeastern Conference's outstanding coach for 1942; in a unique twist, Alexander finished second and Dodd fourth.

Despite Tech's fine record, their home attendance had dropped from 118,000 in 1941 to 87,473, due largely to wartime travel restrictions. Nevertheless, Tech's coffers were healthy enough to cover the $42,736 promised for athletic scholarships for the football team's players and Coach Aleck's salary of $7,200.

Alexander resumed his coaching duties on December 9, making his first visit to the practice field since the Duke game, but only after informing his doctors that he did not intend to live his remaining years as an invalid. He went on to tell them that he had discussed his situation with his wife and family, and everyone agreed that going back to work suited him best. The doctors disagreed; they insisted he give up coaching before the stress killed him.

"If I won't do that, what do you prescribe?" Coach Aleck asked.

Understanding that they were dealing with a stubborn man, the doctors told Coach Aleck he would need to limit his physical activity and change his diet drastically.

"I'll settle for that," Alexander conceded.

Castleberry received the sad news in early December that his close friend Bob Chaffin had been killed in a plane crash in Hawaii on November 29. Chaffin, a lieutenant in the army air corps, had been the student manager at Boys' High when Castleberry played for the Purple Hurricanes. Shortly after hearing the news, Castleberry received a letter written by Chaffin on November 19 and postmarked the day of his death. In it, Chaffin congratulated Castleberry for his fine season and went on to offer a scouting report on the quality of Hawaiian girls. He closed the letter by telling Castleberry he would see him soon. But soon never came.

Thanks in large part to Castleberry's performance that fall, the issue of whether freshmen could play varsity sports was settled in the affirmative. Even Grantland Rice weighed in on the subject in one of his nationally syndicated columns that December, writing, "At least one ancient football belief went overboard with a crash this last fall."

Rice then touted Castleberry's performances and surmised, "What freshmen lack in experience they more than make up in dash and spirit and lack of respect for greater reputations."

The football team's good fortune to be heading to a bowl game came as bad news to Tech's basketball team, which had just begun practicing for the 1943 season and was counting on Castleberry and his fellow football players Wilber Stein, Jack Marshall, Tom Anderson, George Manning, and Pat McHugh.

The status of Castleberry's knee weighed heavily on the football team when practice resumed in advance of the Cotton Bowl. Miraculously, the knee seemed to have healed by Tech's first bowl practice on December 9. Tech trainers taped the knee extensively, and the Jackrabbit ran wild and carefree. During the team's first scrimmage on December 14 against the Red Devils—the scout team—Castleberry broke for a 50-yard touchdown after faking a pass, and all agreed he looked fully recovered. The good fortune did not hold.

Several days before a three-day Christmas break, Castleberry took a hit in practice to his injured knee. The injury wasn't bad enough to relegate him to crutches, but the Tech coaches grew concerned about how effective he would be against Texas. Doctors and coaches agreed that an operation was in order if he wanted to regain full use of his knee, but the operation was put off until after New Year's Day so Castleberry could play against the Longhorns.

News from Texas came that the Longhorns were considering a raid on their freshman team to grab a few players prior to the Cotton Bowl. The Southwest Conference had operated under a no-freshman rule for the 1942 season but had changed its tune at the end of the season. Freshman punter Frank Guess was prominent among the players D.X. Bible was considering for duty. Guess could boom a football high and far, which, in theory, could go a long way toward thwarting Castleberry's punt returns.

Almost comical by today's standards were the rules of decorum expected of Tech football players at a bowl game. Here is a memo Tech players received prior to departing for the Cotton Bowl:

> *Georgia Tech has made trips to two previous bowl games and four intersectional trips for games with the University of California. All of these teams have set a standard of behavior, appearance and general conduct that was very high. This institution has received many compliments from all sections of the country on the appearance and behavior of the Georgia Tech teams in hotels and other public places. We are anxious that this team set an even higher standard under the extremely difficult travel conditions that we are facing at this time.*
>
> *The Georgia Tech teams do not slouch around in corduroy pants and sweaters when on the road. Sports jackets or sports clothes are all right, but we must insist on collar, tie and a shave.*
>
> *I want to emphasize again my standard rule for football teams on the road about gambling. I have no objections to bridge games for no stakes, if they do not last too long. Nothing in the world will break up the morale of a football team as much as a bunch of crapshooters or heavy poker and black jack players. Too long a session at cards exhausts any man mentally and will not leave him keyed for the affair we have on hand, i.e., the game with Texas University.*
>
> *After the game, when you will have two or three days before you get home and when you will be out of training, remember that you will be watched by a great many people. People in the public eye have to be careful about their conduct at all times. Please remember that we expect you to behave like gentlemen or, at the present time I might add, like officers and gentlemen.*
>
> *We are going to attempt to give you just as nice a time on this trip as we consistently can and at the same time be ready for a big football game, and within the limits of good behavior. – W.A. Alexander, Director of Athletics.*

The directive was not without irony. The entire team knew that Dodd, the consummate competitor, loved a game of chance.

Transportation difficulties required Tech to split into three groups for travel on regular trains over two routes to Dallas. One group traveled through New Orleans, while the other two boarded trains that went through Memphis. One of those two actually conducted a light workout in Memphis.

John Crawford rode on the same train with Coach Aleck, who opened eyes with a grand gesture during the trip.

"When we crossed the Mississippi River, Coach Aleck threw the film of the Georgia game into the river," Crawford said. "He went back to the observation car and away it went. We got rid of that one pretty quick."

In accordance with the wishes of the Office of Defense Transportation, tickets sent to Tech for the Cotton Bowl were not sold in the Atlanta area; rather, they were scheduled to be distributed to Tech alumni living in and near Dallas.

Bible continued to praise Tech in advance of the game, noting that Tech used speed and deception more than any team Texas had played. "We're expecting a razzle-dazzle attack from Bill Alexander's boys that will equal anything ever seen in the southwest," said Bible, who also expressed regret that Tech had lost its last game. He predicted that the Yellow Jackets would come out against the Longhorns like a house afire, just as Georgia had done against Tech after losing to Auburn.

Not to be outdone, Coach Aleck lavished praise on the Texas offense. "They must have a million players," Coach Aleck said. "They use the single-wing with the wingback both up and back; they use the double-wing, short punt, and a spread, too. And we don't know a great deal about 'em except what we've learned through other coaches who've played them in recent years. Dana Bible is a very able coach and has done a brilliant job."

Coach Aleck managed to maintain his sense of humor, too, commenting on what Texas had been able to learn after their scout attended Tech's game against Georgia. "I don't think they could have learned much. We didn't have the ball," Coach Aleck said.

Once the Tech team assembled in Dallas, Coach Aleck's first order of business was to make sure the team had not gone "soft" over the holidays, because, as Coach Aleck explained, "looking at the whites of his team's eyes," he could tell they were in need of some hard work. The team's first full workout in Dallas took place at a high school football field, and the sole intent of the practice was to run off all the food the players had eaten during their Christmas hiatus. The Yellow Jackets were greeted by a blue norther for their first practice, making conditions icy and biting cold.

Describing the Texas team the week of the game, Ed Danforth of *The Atlanta Journal* reached into the bag of politically incorrect metaphors that typified the time:

"The Southwestern champions, gentlemen, are typical examples of the progeny of the pioneers who knocked the noble Red Man for a loop and took his grazing lands away from him."

Texas had led nation in defense in 1942 by limiting its opponents to just 117.3 yards of total offense per game. Not to be outdone, the Longhorns' offense had led the nation the previous year and boasted such big, fast players as bruising All-Southwest Conference backs Roy Dale McKay and Jackie Field, who weighed 198 and 190 pounds, respectively. Max Minor, a 205-pounder with speed, also played in the Longhorns' backfield. Field and Minor could each cover 100 yards in 9.8 seconds and had been integral cogs in the Longhorn track team's standout sprint relay.

Castleberry spoke for his teammates when asked about Tech's chances against the talented Texas team.

"We feel that we can redeem ourselves for the defeat by Georgia if we take Texas," Castleberry said.

Dodd was less optimistic, lamenting that he could not figure out what was wrong with the team. He wondered aloud if they had played their best football in November, because they had looked anything but sharp while preparing to meet the Longhorns.

The blue norther had passed through Dallas by New Year's Day, unveiling pristine weather conditions when the Cotton Bowl kicked off on a Friday afternoon with a partisan Texas crowd of 36,000 in attendance. Tech wore blue jerseys, gray pants, and black helmets, giving their uniforms a similar look to those worn by Rice, the team that most reminded Bible of Tech.

From the outset, Texas' line size posed problems for the smaller Tech line, but the Longhorns weren't able to get anything going until midway through the first quarter, when they recovered Bill McHugh's fumble. The turnover sparked a 12-play Texas drive, and the Longhorns cashed in when McKay spotted Minor in the end zone with Castleberry covering. He delivered the pass and Castleberry managed to deflect it, but Minor hauled in the deflection just before going out of bounds to put Texas up by a touchdown. According to the contingent of Atlanta sportswriters covering the game, the Texas receiver had caught the ball out of bounds.

Tech went into halftime trailing 7 – 0. In the Tech locker room underneath the Cotton Bowl stands, a moving scene unfolded.

"Coach Aleck came in and gave us a handshake and bid us good bye," John Crawford said. "And he hoped the best for us, and that sort of thing. What he was talking about was that we were leaving there and going to war. Coach Aleck was a great fellow and a good football coach, but he wasn't the kind of fellow who would snuggle up to you all the time. He was pretty tough. So that was sort of a tearjerker."

Castleberry's knee continued to bother him. He had barely been able to walk the week before the game, and now it was clearly affecting his performance. Despite reports of the injury, Texas respected Castleberry as if he could break free at any moment, as evidenced by the way the Longhorns worked to keep the ball away from him on punts.

Tech would have been wise to extend the same respect to the speedy Field, Texas' return man. Trailing 7 – 0 in the third quarter, Tech punted to Field, who caught the punt at his own 40 and went the distance, putting Texas ahead 14 – 0.

Texas' massive line allowed Field, Minor, and McKay to pound through the Tech defense for big gains, and the same linemen on defense unleashed a rush the likes of which Tech had not seen all season. In the second quarter they penetrated Tech's line and threw Castleberry for losses of 13 and 7 yards on consecutive plays while he looked for an open receiver. If the Jackrabbit's knee had been healthy, he might have sidestepped the Texas rush as he had done so many times during the season, but he was hobbled. While the Longhorns dominated play, they weren't able to put away their scrappy opponent from the Southeastern Conference. Unlike the Georgia game, when Tech simply had nothing to give, Tech didn't surrender under the weight of the two-touchdown deficit. Early in the fourth quarter, Castleberry finally got his hands on a Texas punt and almost broke free for a long return. Again the knee seemed to restrict his movement, and he failed to execute a last maneuver into open space. Instead, Texas collared him at the Tech 33.

Tech then went to work and began to march up the field, however, thanks to Castleberry's left arm. Though his knee was bad, his throwing arm was not, and he riddled the Longhorns' secondary with passes. Facing a fourth and goal at the Texas 4, Eddie Prokop took the snap and went back as if to pass. Then David Eldredge swept behind him to take the football and scoot around the left side into the end zone, giving Tech one final successful Statue of Liberty play.

Minutes later, Texas again had to punt. Trying to keep the ball away from Castleberry, their punter kicked the ball out of bounds at the Tech 46, where Castleberry began to lead another drive. Tech marched to the Texas 3, but the Longhorns held. Taking over with three minutes to play, Texas then kept the football until time ran out to preserve a 14 – 7 win. Clint Castleberry's team had lost for the second time in his football career, and Tech had suffered its first bowl defeat in three tries.

Farther west in Pasadena, Georgia defeated UCLA 9 – 0 to win the Rose Bowl and become national champions. In Miami, Alabama put to rest any notion that Northeast football had an edge on the rest of the country, taking a convincing 37 – 21 win over Boston College.

20

Winter of the Crazed Jackrabbit

Doctors performed surgery on Clint Castleberry's injured knee at Atlanta's Crawford Long Hospital on February 2, 1943. Afterward, the doctors announced that they expected the young man to make a full recovery.

Meanwhile, the city of Atlanta had continued to look for ways to help support the war effort and had come up with the idea of what amounted to a football party at Atlanta's exclusive Ansley Hotel. Sponsored jointly by *The Atlanta Constitution*, Georgia Tech, and the University of Georgia, the January gala offered attendees a chance to mingle with Tech and Georgia players, the list of whom included Castleberry and Charley Trippi, and to view films of the Rose, Cotton, and Orange bowls. Coach Wally Butts was there too, but Coach Aleck could not attend due to his health. Bobby Dodd tried to attend but could not find transportation from Florida to reach the event in time.

Tickets for the party were determined by the value of war bonds purchased at special booths in the Atlanta Athletic Club and department stores throughout Atlanta, such as Rich's and Davison-Paxon. The choicest seats went to those purchasing bonds of

$1,000, and the next best seats were reserved for those buying bonds of $500. The cheap seats went for bonds of $100.

Bonds sold for the event were earmarked to build the new *Atlanta* to replace the cruiser sunk at Guadalcanal. By the end of the evening, the bowl bond gala had registered a total sale of $1,028,800. Jack Troy wrote in *The Atlanta Constitution*, "This is the kind of spirit that lures Axis rats into death-dealing traps."

In February, Castleberry and seventeen Tech teammates were called into service in the army air corps. They went willingly to fight what they considered a necessary war against evil enemies.

"We wanted to go," said Bob Sheldon, who joined the marines. "It's like Clint, he could have stayed in school. It was all 'kill a Jap' or 'kill a German.' Of course, the media did a good job of selling that."

Castleberry withdrew from school on February 18 and departed for Miami, Florida, on February 22 to begin training to be a pilot.

＊ ＊ ＊ ＊ ＊

Army doctors examined Castleberry's knee and reported that he was recovering nicely. The injury would not keep him from flying. Once Castleberry's military commitment was over, he looked forward to returning to Tech and finishing his football career. But he did not want to shortchange his military service by taking the easy way out.

"He was definitely going to go do his part," Shirley Poole said. "Some people are very heroic. They told him he could teach or make appearances in front of the boys—the servicemen—and so forth, about football. But no, he thought it was great to go on and become an aviation cadet."

As it turned out, Castleberry found familiar faces in Miami Beach. Many of his Tech teammates were part of the same contingent, including Don Paschal.

"We went to Miami when we left Atlanta and Tech, to get acclimated to the training of the air force. It seemed like the whole team was there," John Crawford said. "Clint was along. Everybody who was going into the service went to the same destination. The military took over all the big hotels down in Miami at that time and turned them over to the air force. The army got in there, too. They just made it army property to take care of people like us who were down there for training. There were no civilians there at that time. They were all trainees."

Tech's Miami bunch had college football contemporaries in the neighborhood, too, in the form of a large contingent of Mississippi State players who were housed at the same location. The natural SEC rivalry led to "The Jeep Bowl" touch football competition between the two factions, which they played on a large field near Miami Beach. Castleberry continued to recover from his knee surgery and did not participate in the games, but he always showed up to support his Tech brethren.

In March 1943, Secretary of the Navy Frank Knox received a check from John L. Connor, chairman of the City of Atlanta's war bond selling campaign, for $63 million—enough to build the new USS *Atlanta*.

Trainees such as Castleberry were a part of CTD, the College Training Detachment, and were dispatched to various destinations to learn how to fly. Once they became qualified pilots, some were directed to become fighter or single-engine pilots, while others became bomber pilots.

Castleberry's next assignment was to Centre College in Danville, Kentucky, in the spring of 1943. His new orders came at approximately the same time as the NFL draft, in which the Detroit Lions selected Frankie Sinkwich with the first pick. The marine corps rejected the young man recognized as the country's finest college football player due to physical reasons, but those same physical problems did not trouble the NFL.

In late August, Castleberry was transferred to the Army Air Classification Center in Nashville, Tennessee, where, coincidentally, he was joined by Paschal and three other former teammates from Boys' High: Joe Kenimer, Gordon Clay, and Ralph Carroll. Approximately a month later, on September 20, 1943, three weeks shy of his twentieth birthday, Castleberry married Shirley Poole in the post chapel. In an Associated Press photo from the ceremony, the couple's youth make them look more like Archie and Veronica at the malt shop than a bride and groom. The glows on their youthful faces suggest that each is envisioning a future of days as grand as their wedding day.

By November 1943, all of the "Boys' High Five" had been transferred to Maxwell Field pre-flight school in Montgomery, Alabama.
Castleberry felt that military training was preparing him well for his
return to Tech after fulfilling his obligation.

"I'm in good shape," Castleberry told The Associated Press.
"And I will be as long as I'm in the army air forces. Those 17-year-
old athletes now signing up with the Air Corps Enlisted Reserve
ought to be tops in sports after the war. They'll be rugged and
they'll be men."

Clint's rigorous schedule didn't leave a lot of time to spend with
Shirley, even if they were married. From Montgomery, Castleberry
went to Lafayette, Louisiana, then made several stops in Arkansas
for further training.

"It was cadet training," Shirley said. "You would live for the
weekends. And we'd go up there to a little town and not have too
much money. We'd have a room at a place that was not quite a
boarding house. There would be families who would take in a couple of aviation cadets and their wives. On Friday nights, we'd get an
ice cream cone and we'd walk back to where we lived."

Looking past his return to the football field after the war,
Castleberry also had ideas about coaching. No doubt playing for
the likes of Shorty Doyal, Coach Aleck, and Bobby Dodd played a
big part in shaping his mindset while also grooming him well for
that future possibility.

"The idea of being a coach seemed to suit him," Shirley said.
"He wanted to coach young players the way he had been coached."

Castleberry returned to Atlanta in July 1944 shortly after
receiving his wings to earn the rank of lieutenant. During his visit
he attended the first annual banquet of the Boys' High Alumni and
Athletic Association at the Biltmore Hotel. Also in attendance after
earning their wings were Castleberry's Boys' High teammates
Jimmy Gordon, Paschal, and Clay. Each expected to be shipped
overseas for combat duty at any moment.

*   *   *   *   *

The excitement generated by the Jackrabbit's performances in the
Midwest and Annapolis had helped college football survive.
Through the magic of radio and accounts in newspapers across the

country, the wee freshman had captured the imagination of a nation. Despite all the uncertainties, college football headed into the 1943 season with the solid backing of a country that considered the sport to be woven into its DNA.

Entering the 1943 season, few college football coaches had any idea which players would be on their rosters to compete that fall. Colleges continued to operate around the year, holding full slates of classes during the summer so students could graduate early for military service. All any coach could do was to scout which players were in school and speculate which of those might still be available once the new season kicked off. The football teams of schools fortunate enough to have military training facilities were forecast to become powerhouses, since they alone would benefit from the enrollment of military personnel in training.

Though Castleberry would not play for Georgia Tech in 1943, there were reasons to believe that Tech's football program would remain at the top. Tech got a lot of good players through the school's Navy V-12 program, which derived from the navy's overwhelming need for competent officers to direct its growing forces. The Naval Academy simply could not train all the officers needed.

More than 100,000 men would be enrolled in the V-12 program at United States colleges and universities between July 1943 and June 1946. In addition to educating future military leaders, the V-12 program helped America's colleges and universities survive the loss of existing and potential students to enlistment and the draft. Those selected for the V-12 program operated almost as if they were already in the military before moving on to Naval Reserve midshipmen's school or marine corps boot camp, followed by the Officer Candidate Course. After training, they were commissioned as navy ensigns or marine corps second lieutenants.

* * * * *

Coach Aleck coached Tech in 1943 and 1944, leading the Yellow Jackets to Sugar and Orange bowl appearances, but his health forced him to retire prior to the 1945 season, and Dodd took over to become the third head football coach in Tech history.

Lt. Clint Castleberry shipped out to the Mediterranean Theater in the fall of 1944. He had wanted to fly a P-51 Mustang Fighter but instead became co-pilot on a B-26G Marauder bomber known as "Dream Girl." He was stationed in Africa. Shortly before his departure, Clint found out that he would be a father. Sixty-seven years later, Shirley remembered her husband's reaction upon learning of her pregnancy.

"He was thrilled to death," she said. "We were so excited. That was a special moment. He looked forward to being a father. I knew he would be a good one, too. He was such a nice person."

After Clint went overseas, Shirley returned to Atlanta, moved in with her parents, and took a job at Rich's department store, working several days a week.

*   *   *   *   *

On November 7, 1944, American voters elected Franklin Delano Roosevelt to an unprecedented fourth term in the White House. Also on that day, an American submarine, the U.S.S. *Albacore,* hit a mine and exploded days after refueling at Midway in the Pacific. Eighty-five men died on the submarine, which had sunk 13 ships during her first ten patrols. Only later—when enemy information solved the mystery—did the navy learn what had happened to the submarine, which had been presumed lost when it had not returned to Midway by December 21.

Another mystery from that day would never be solved, however. At approximately 2:20 A.M. Atlanta time, two B-26G Marauder bombers took off from Roberts Field in Liberia, where the time was 7:20 A.M. The bombers' mission was to continue a ferrying run up the coast of Africa toward Dakar, Senegal. Castleberry served as co-pilot for one of the bombers, which also carried a pilot and three other crewmen. Two hours later, both planes disappeared.

For six days American and Royal Air Force aircraft and Royal Navy ships searched the area where the planes were believed to have collided and fallen into the sea, between Isle de Orango and Dakar. One small British marine craft did spot a fuel cell from an American aircraft, but they could not haul back the debris for further examination.

Castleberry's last letter home had a Liberia postmark and was dated November 6, 1944. On November 19, Shirley's father called her at work with the bad news.

"My daddy was the one who told me a telegraph had arrived at the house, telling me he was missing in action," said Shirley, who was four months into her pregnancy. "But you had the feeling he might show up. He just couldn't be gone. It just didn't seem possible."

The Atlanta Constitution reported the news in its November 20 edition, which also featured a story about Frankie Sinkwich throwing four touchdowns to lead the Detroit Lions to a 41 – 21 win over the Chicago Bears.

Shorty Doyal remained hopeful that the best player he had ever coached might still be alive. He told *The Atlanta Constitution,* "If Clint had half a chance he'll show up yet. He was one of the hardest battlers I ever saw. He hated to lose worse than anyone, and his aggressiveness will bring him back if there is the slightest chance. It is surely tragic to think that such fine boys as Clint Castleberry can be sacrificed to the Gods of War."

Paschal, who was finishing his Air Force training at Fort Bragg, North Carolina, and Kenimer, who had become a pilot on a four-engine bomber, believed Castleberry had been forced down and that eventually he would be heard from again. Neither could believe their friend and former teammate could be dead.

Paschal reflected on a touching letter he'd received from his friend prior to his departure from the States. In the letter, Castleberry had addressed their lives and friendship in addition to expressing his happiness about becoming a father. Frustrated and broken-hearted, Paschal could only express how much he wished he could have switched fates with his friend.

On November 23, 1944, a telegraph arrived from the U.S. War Department indicating that Castleberry's status had been changed from "missing in action" to "killed in action," based on unidentified wreckage spotted by an RAF plane.

"The two planes disappeared," Shirley said. "The [army] never did give us any satisfaction about what had happened, other than the two planes disappeared and that Clint had been a co-pilot. They never reached where they were supposed to be going. They disappeared off the African coast. They were going up to France I suppose. They didn't say exactly."

Tech's football team received the news about their teammate a day before losing 21 – 0 to Notre Dame in Atlanta, where, according to *The Chicago Daily Tribune*, "the gayety attending tomorrow's game and Georgia Tech's invitation to the Orange Bowl was offset on the campus by news that Clint Castleberry, the Yellow Jackets famed halfback of 1942, had been killed in action in the European war theater."

Sheldon was with the marines on Guam when he received the news about Castleberry.

"We were staging for Iwo Jima," Sheldon said. "I had lost a brother in October the same way, missing in action. He was in a B-24. Those things happened in those days. And you don't know why. I guess he was the co-pilot, and I always felt if he'd been the pilot, he'd have probably pulled it out."

Shirley shared Sheldon's view that if Clint had been the pilot, his fate might have been different. "He was just classified as a co-pilot," Shirley said. "I don't know if it would have made a bit of difference, but if he'd been the pilot, he might have had more of a chance."

That line of thinking did have merit given Castleberry's extraordinary reflexes, instinctive responses, and ability to perform in the clutch. If anybody could have stared down disaster and cheated death, the Jackrabbit was that young man.

Shirley did manage to attain one morsel of information that supports the theory that the two planes did indeed run into each other.

"I can still remember somebody saying that the pilot of the other plane said on the radio, 'The sun's in my eyes, get over,'" Shirley said. "You just had to think that if Clint had been the pilot, he could have done something."

Even though Castleberry had been officially declared dead by the army, funeral services were never held. "I guess nobody could believe he wasn't coming back," Shirley said. "That's the reason. That was sad, but I think that's how everybody wanted to feel. There was not a lot of hope, even though Clint's parents and I thought he might have survived and that he was running around on a beach somewhere. But there was not much hope. Mr. Castleberry and I were the only ones who continued to believe he was alive."

Epilogue

Two years after Clint Castleberry had gone to Athens, Georgia to play against the University of Georgia, and almost a month-after receiving news of his disappearance, Tech's 1944 squad played the team that cost them their undefeated season in 1942. Their hearts heavy with the loss of their fallen friend and former teammate, Tech went out and defeated Georgia 44 – 0. Bobby Dodd coached the game for Coach Aleck, who could not travel due to continued poor health. Frank Broyles, who had been a freshman at Tech with Castleberry, threw three touchdown passes and ran for two more in the rout. Broyles, like Castleberry, dreamed of one day becoming a football coach, and he did just that, coaching at several stops before becoming the head coach at the University of Arkansas, where he became a coaching legend.

To this day, Georgia does not count the 1944 loss to Tech in their record book. Tech had a heavy infusion of Navy V-12 trainees in their squad, and Georgia did not. Tech does include the 1944 win—which was Tech's first in Athens since 1906—in their rivalry ledger. Then again, heated rivals rarely agree on anything.

Georgia Tech students spearheaded a campaign of alumni, faculty, and fans of Georgia Tech to raise money for a memorial fund for Clint Castleberry, football hero and fallen aviator. The result was a $4,079,100 war bond purchase made in his honor.

By August 1945, more than 800 college varsity, professional, and nationally ranked amateur athletes had given their lives in the service of their country since Pearl Harbor. Included in that number was Niles Kinnick, the University of Iowa's All-America halfback, who died in the Caribbean when his plane failed to return to its carrier. Star miler Lou Zamperini, remembered for climbing a flagpole and stealing a swastika at the 1936 Berlin Olympics, was killed in action in the South Pacific, and Charlie Paddock, the famed Olympic sprinter whose participation in the 1928 Olympics was a part of the storyline for the 1981 Oscar-winning movie *Chariots of Fire*, died in an air crash while serving in the marines.

Castleberry wasn't the only casualty from his disappearance on the other side of the world. Clint's father never recovered from the loss of his son.

"My father never gave up hope that he was alive—that somehow they'd gone down close enough to land, and Clint was somewhere in Africa," Jimmy Castleberry told *The Atlanta Journal-Constitution* in 1989. "For many, many, many years, he held onto the barest hope."

Clinton Castleberry Sr. died in 1961, still clinging to the hope, even 17 years later, that his son had somehow survived.

Shirley Dillon Clinton was born on April 21, 1945, to a mother still reeling from a great loss, a young widow with a child.

"It was easier for me to believe that he was coming back for several years," Shirley said. "It was such a shock. It was a great shock, really. I felt like he was not dead. I did not think he had died. In fact it took me several years before I came to terms with that. I don't even know how to describe it. I can't believe how long it was before I accepted that he wasn't coming home."

Many nights after getting her baby to sleep and settling into sleep herself, Clint would live in her dreams.

"I had a recurring dream where I could see him running around on a beach," Shirley said. "I think when you feel so strongly about something like that, your imagination goes wild."

Shirley never became a librarian, but she eventually moved on with her life. She married Frederick Avey approximately five years after Clint's disappearance. Avey graduated from Georgia Tech as a civil engineer, and the couple settled down in St. Louis and had three daughters.

"I've been very fortunate," Shirley said.

Fred died in 1995. Shirley still lives in St. Louis, where the passage of time has made Clint Castleberry a cherished but distant memory to his loving widow. Every now and then, though, she'll see

*Clint Castleberry's brother, Jimmy, was a member of two state champ-
ionship teams at Boys' High and followed his brother to Georgia
Tech.*

an old black-and-white movie that she saw first with Clint, or she'll
hear an old, familiar Glenn Miller tune, and the memories become
vivid again of young sweethearts in love.

Mary Okron Stimmel's family lived in a house in Atlanta that
was built in 1939 and first occupied by Clint Castleberry's family.

"When we first moved here we had some kind of ghostly ema-
nations, and we're not real ghost seekers at all," said Stimmel in an
interview conducted by the Georgia Tech Department of Living
History.

Stimmel recounted hearing noises from inside her bedroom
closet, and her daughter had experienced some things in her room
that were "a little bit frightening." Then, on a Sunday morning,
Stimmel's husband thought he heard Mary go running down the
stairs, go out the front door, and slam the door behind her. Figuring she had gone out to get the paper, he began to fix breakfast, but

he didn't see his wife. Finally, he walked back upstairs and found his wife still sleeping in bed.

"And he told me about this, and I said, 'whatever' you know," Mary said.

On the following Monday, Mary listened to WGST on the radio while driving home from work.

"They were saying spring practice [at Georgia Tech] had started the day before," Mary said. "So I came home and said to Carl, I think I know who that was."

Mary cited another incident that took place while her son was playing a board game in the dining room and listening to a Glenn Miller record.

"The song was 'Don't Sit Under the Apple Tree,' and it played, stopped, and started over again," Mary said. "This was not a CD. This was an old record. And we've had other events happen like that."

Mary and her family were convinced that Clint Castleberry was a constant visitor to his old house. "I do feel like he is sometimes around here," Mary said. "I still find it confounding."

Boys' High and Tech High continued to be Atlanta's favored matchup of the fall through the 1946 game, which was played in front of 23,000 at Grant Field. Tech High won the final game to secure an 18 games to 15 games advantage in the series, which included a 13 – 13 tie in 1944. After the 1946 contest, the series that had begun in 1912 came to an end due to the restructuring of Atlanta's school system.

Shorty Doyal moved on to Atlanta's Marist High School, where he coached through 1951, carrying a composite record of 230 – 73 – 14 into retirement.

Today, the grounds where Boys' High and Tech High stood are a part of Grady High School. The Boys' High Alumni Association had an arch built in front of the school that was dedicated on May 22, 2002. "Grady High" is scrolled across the top of the arch, but a plaque on the front wall commemorates the existence of Boys' High.

Mack Tharpe, the former Tech line coach, achieved his dream of becoming a navy pilot at the age of 41, flying torpedo bombers while serving on the carrier *Bismarck Sea*. Initially the carrier had been named *Alikula Bay,* but it was renamed to honor a memorable Allied naval victory on the Bismarck Sea northeast of New Guinea. On February 21, 1945, Japanese kamikaze pilots struck the carrier and caused enough damage to sink the vessel. Tharpe was last seen helping his men into life rafts while his ship sank.

George Poschner never had trouble displaying his mettle on a football field for the University of Georgia, and those same qualities translated well to combat. Serving as an army infantry officer in the European Theater, Poschner epitomized courage and heroism. During the Battle of the Bulge, he attacked an enemy machine gun placement that was blocking a vital road, spraying submachine gun fire on the enemy as he advanced through a hail of bullets and killing or wounding at least twenty Germans along the way. They were the toughest yards he'd ever run, and they were the last. Having closed to 30 yards of the enemy machine gun, Poschner took a bullet to his head and was presumed dead. His troops continued forward in the freezing cold, and the fighting continued over the next three days until the Americans regained control of the area. That's when medical personnel found Poschner. A bullet had passed through the front of his eye and out the back of his head, yet he still had a pulse. The polar temperatures had helped him survive but also brought frostbite that caused him to lose the fingers on his right hand. Gangrene prompted amputations of both legs below the knees. The bullet to the head brought paralysis to his left side.

Frankie Sinkwich played for the Lions for two seasons, twice earning All-Pro honors and winning the Most Valuable Player award in 1944. He joined the air force in 1945 and incurred a knee injury while playing for the air force football team that was serious enough to end his playing career at the age of 25. After coaching football at Furman, South Carolina, and the University of Tampa, Sinkwich turned his attention to becoming a businessman and enjoyed success as a wholesale beer distributor. He died of cancer on October 22, 1990.

Charley Trippi spent almost three years in the air force before returning to the University of Georgia to resume his football career.

"Sure, I had some disappointment at what the war did to my football career at Georgia," Trippi said. "But what were you going to do? Everybody was in the same boat and a lot of them didn't come home. I just had to get back out there and start over again."

Trippi returned in time to play six games for Georgia during the 1945 season, then served as a captain on Georgia's undefeated SEC championship team in 1946, earning All-America honors and winning the Maxwell Award. Army's Glenn Davis edged out Trippi for the Heisman Trophy.

Trippi flawlessly moved into the ranks of the NFL to play for the Chicago Cardinals (today's Arizona Cardinals); he also played a season of minor league baseball, where he advanced as high as Class AA before focusing on professional football. Trippi's nine-year career ended in 1955, and he was enshrined in the Pro Football Hall of Fame in 1968.

Wally Butts coached Georgia to Southeastern Conference championships in 1946, 1948, and 1959. In 21 seasons he posted a 140 – 86 – 9 record, which included a bowl record of 5 – 2 – 1. He stepped down as the Bulldogs' coach after the 1960 season but remained the school's athletic director until 1963.

Of note, Butts filed a libel suit against the *Saturday Evening Post*, which had run an article entitled "The Story of a College Football Fix," written by Frank Graham Jr. In the article, Graham's main source, an Atlanta businessman, alleged that he had been accidentally hooked into a telephone conversation between Butts and his friend, famed Alabama coach Paul "Bear" Bryant. During that conversation, Butts was said to have passed on secrets to Bryant prior to a September 22, 1962 Georgia – Alabama game. Alabama had been a 17-point favorite and won the game 35 – 0 over a Georgia team coached by Butts's successor, Johnny Griffith. Butts and Bryant each sued for $10 million. Bryant settled for $300,000, while Butts moved forward with his suit. *Curtis Publishing Co. v. Butts* became a landmark libel case when an Atlanta jury award Butts $3.06 million. The judge decided the award was too steep and lowered the amount to $460,000. The Curtis Publishing Company appealed, but on October 9, 1967, the United States Supreme Court decided not to hear the case. The *Post* paid Butts eight days later. Even though the amount had been reduced to $460,000, it contributed largely to Curtis Publishing's decision to quit publishing the *Post* in 1969.

Butts died in 1973.

On April 23, 1950, Coach Aleck's family awakened but did not find him camped in the sitting room reading the newspaper. So his wife went to his room, where she found him in bed with the look of a man in a blissful sleep. His heart was no longer beating. Sometime that night, a final coronary occlusion had occurred. Coach Aleck was gone.

In the wake of Coach Aleck's passing, Walter Stewart, the sports editor of the Memphis *Commercial Appeal* wrote the following:

"Old Alex was a sort of synonym for Georgia Tech—the very texture of the school's personality—tough cement between the stones of battlements brave with White and Gold.

"Death called gently to William A. Alexander in the first gray light of Sunday—broke another link binding us to a gracious and gallant past. For he had been the core of Georgia Tech athletic destiny through 40 years of harsh combat. He had symbolized the dignity and honor of Southern football and a great emptiness surges behind him. He led without fear and asked no quarter. He leaves a memorial built in the lives of those who served him."

Georgia Tech's Alexander Memorial Coliseum is named after Coach Aleck.

Bobby Dodd took over for Coach Aleck in 1945, ushering in what is generally regarded as the golden era of Georgia Tech football. Perceived as the gentleman coach, Dodd continued to dance to his own tune, never seeing a reason to make football anything more than fun for his players. He never held long practices. He believed that if a player couldn't understand what he was being taught in a practice that lasted less than two hours, he wasn't about to get it by sticking around for three. Putting away the footballs for the evening and getting back after it the next day was Dodd's answer.

His practices were short, but his list of team rules might have been even shorter. He did not allow alcohol, and he wanted all of his players to attend church regularly, though he did not care what church they chose to attend. He didn't mind if a player wanted to smoke, as long as he did not do so in public, nor did he mind players having girls in the their rooms or getting married—things many colleges did not put up with during that era of coaching. Dodd even allowed girlfriends or wives to attend practices and sit on the bench.

He felt that nothing made one of his players feel better than to walk off the field with his girl hanging on one arm.

Pepper Rodgers, the young boy who idolized Castleberry, played quarterback for Georgia Tech under Dodd. In addition, Rodgers took care of kicking duties and made 39 extra points in 1952 to establish a single-season mark that stood for 38 years.

Rodgers kicked the winning field goal in the final minutes of the 1952 Orange Bowl to lead Tech to a 17 – 14 win over Baylor. He also won the Sugar Bowl's Most Valuable Player award in 1954 when the Yellow Jackets defeated West Virginia 42 – 19. In 1974, Rodgers became the sixth head football coach in Georgia Tech history.

"Bobby Dodd certainly would not have been described as a hard ass," Rodgers said. "He'd be described as a fair man who would tell guys, 'have a good time after the game, just don't embarrass yourself.' The fact that he did a lot of things other coaches didn't do allowed him to attract some players that he might not otherwise have gotten to attend Georgia Tech. He was a very good and obviously successful football coach."

Preparing for bowl games did not change Dodd's approach. Many college teams worked through the Christmas break to get ready for New Year's Day battles. Dodd allowed his teams to go home once they took their final exams in the fall. They would resume practicing once they reached the host city for whatever bowl they were playing in, at which point Dodd wanted his players to enjoy the sights and sounds of the city. In bowl practices he drilled his teams on being penalty-free, holding on to the football, and winning the kicking game. Judging from Dodd's nine wins in 13 bowl games, his philosophy of getting a team ready for the big game worked.

Dodd remained Tech's head coach from 1945 through 1966, compiling a record of 165 – 64 – 8. Highlights from those years included the period from 1952 to 1956, when he coached Tech to six consecutive bowl wins: one Orange Bowl, one Cotton Bowl, three Sugar Bowls, and one Gator Bowl.

Dodd enjoyed a 31-game unbeaten streak from 1951 – 53, which included a 12 – 0 team in 1952. And perhaps most endearing to Tech fans was the fact that he was the coach who led Tech to eight consecutive wins over archrival Georgia from 1949 through 1956.

Bobby Dodd, the third head football coach in Georgia Tech history,
is shown here in the fall of 1966, his final season of coaching.

Tech games possessed an alluring intangible during the Dodd
years. In a city without professional sports, Saturday afternoons in
Atlanta belonged to Georgia Tech while Dodd created the magic,
calling the shots from the sideline.

"He was obviously a great competitor and I think ahead of his
time in things that he did," Rodgers said. "Coach Dodd wasn't
afraid of hiring good people, and they helped him achieve his goals.
The thing most all of the players liked about Coach Dodd was that
he took care of the players. When the players would finish their

eligibility, he would keep them on [scholarship] until they graduated as long as they were making any kind of progress. And obviously, he was a very sound football coach. In those days kicking was a big part of the game—punting and quick kicking—and Coach Dodd used that to his great advantage. And he had a much more sound knowledge of the kicking game than most people."

After retiring from coaching following the 1967 Orange Bowl, Dodd continued as Georgia Tech's athletic director until 1976. Throughout that time, Dodd kept an enlarged photograph of Clint Castleberry hanging on the wall of his office. To Dodd, the photograph remained a source of inspiration until he died of cancer on June 21, 1988.

"He was the boy every father wanted his son to be," said Dodd of Castleberry.

In 1988, Georgia Tech's Grant Field was renamed Bobby Dodd Stadium at Historic Grant Field.

Clint Castleberry remains a mythical figure on the Georgia Tech campus. Dodd eulogized Castleberry by saying that if he hadn't joined the war, he would have been "the greatest player in Tech history" and would surely have been "an All-American for his remaining three years."

He finished by saying, "He was a great boy: gentle and brave, manly, yet sweet."

In the poem "To an Athlete Dying Young," A.E. Houseman wrote:

Now you will not swell the rout

Of lads that wore their honour out,

Runners whom renown outran

And the name died before the man.

Clint Castleberry's name has never died. To this day, his number 19 remains the only football jersey Georgia Tech has ever retired.

Acknowledgments

Coming from a Georgia Tech family, I heard Clint Castleberry's name when I was too young to understand his significance. But I never forgot the name, and once I became a sportswriter, I yearned to learn more about him. That desire led me to write this narrative about his life and the period in which he thrived. Information about Castleberry did not come easily—there was no Internet in 1942, and many of his contemporaries had died. I conducted many hours of research on the period in which Castleberry lived and accounts of his exploits. In addition, I spent many hours looking for people who had known him, which was difficult given the passage of time since his death. In the end, however, I feel confident in saying that this is the most complete accounting of Castleberry in existence. I feel honored to have been granted the chance to tell the Jackrabbit's story.

A lot of people helped this project come together, beginning with Tris Coburn, who believed in the idea from the first time I mentioned it to him. The Georgia Tech Department of Living History was unbelievable, especially its director, Marilyn Somers. Thanks, Marilyn. My good friend Charlie Britton came through with helpful information that hit me at just the right time, and Jim Elliott and Jim Henry came up big. Bob Graham, my mentor, continues to dispatch strong guidance, and I'm forever grateful to him for taking an interest in me. And a special thanks to Jonathan Eaton for the wonderful job he did editing the manuscript.

Thanks to all of Castleberry's former teammates and classmates from Boys' High, and those from Georgia Tech, who helped bring him to life with their memories and stories.

Special thanks go out to Shirley Avey for showing great patience while I picked her brain about her long-ago husband Clint Castleberry.

Thanks to my late father, Norman Chastain, who first got me interested in this story. When Dad played football on the Tech Jayvee team he had an encounter with a cranky Coach Aleck over a towel, a story that came more alive once I came to know Coach Aleck while writing this book. Thanks also to Mom—you continue to support me all the time—and to Buddy and Tommy: nobody ever had better brothers.

Finally, to my family, Patti, Carly, and Kel, special thanks for your patience over the years. There have been a lot of times I wanted to be there when I could not. I love you all dearly.

Sources

Interviews

Avey, Shirley. August 14, 2009, August 17, 2009, and November 4, 2009.

Crawford, John. August 6, 2009, August 17, 2009, and November 30, 2009.

Daniel, Joseph. Aug. 4, 2009.

Furchgott, M.H. Aug. 3, 2009 and September 22, 2009.

Maffett, Phillip. August 7, 2009.

Rodgers, Pepper. February 6, 2007 and October 23, 2009.

Sheldon, Bob. March 6, 2007 and November 30, 2009.

Skinner, Arthur Chester. Transcript provided by Georgia Tech Department of Living History.

Stimmel, Mary. Transcript provided by Georgia Tech Department of Living History.

Trippi, Charley. Feb. 3, 2009.

Books

Camp, Edwin, *Alexander of Georgia Tech.* Georgia Institute of Technology, 1950.

Cohane, Tim, *Great College Football Coaches of the Twenties and Thirties.* Arlington House, 1973

The Georgia Tech National Alumni Association, *Griffin – You are a great disappointment to me. The tales of Georgia Tech's Dean Emeritus George C. Griffin.* 1971.

Goodwin, George, Herbert Miller, and Anya Martin, *Boys' High Forever: The History of an Extraordinary Atlanta Public High School.* Boys' High Alumni Association, 2006.

Greenspan, Bud, *Play It Again Bud.* Peter H. Wyden, Inc., 1973.

Griessman, B. Eugene, Sara Evelyn Jackson, and Annibel Jenkins, *Images and Memories: Georgia Tech, 1895 – 1985.* The Georgia Tech Foundation, 1985.

Mell, Patrick Hues Jr., *Life of Patrick Hues Mell.* Baptist Book Concern, 1895. (Contains University of Georgia and Georgia Tech background.)

Silver, Murray, *Tech's Luck.* Continental Shelf Publishing (Savannah, Georgia), 2010.

Thorny, Al, *The Ramblin' Wreck: A Story of Georgia Tech Football.* Strode Publications, 1973.

Van Brimmer, Adam, *Stadium Stories: Georgia Tech Yellow Jackets.* Globe Pequot, 2006.

Wallace, Robert B., *The 1966 Yellow Jackets.* Sports Publications, 1967.

Wilkinson, Jack, *Dodd's Luck.* Golden Coast Publishing Company, 1987.

Periodicals

Asher, Gene, "The Ultimate Rivalry." The Magazine of Georgia Business & Politics, July 2006.

Georgia Tech football media guide, 2002.

McMurry, Richard M., "Clint Castleberry, Coach Alex and the 1942 Team of Destiny." College Football Historical Society Newsletter, Vol. VI, Number III, May 1993.

Overman, Leslie, "Firearms Should Be Deposited With the Professor in Charge." Georgia Tech Alumni Magazine, January/February 2011.

The Saturday Evening Post, various articles/issues.

Sports Illustrated, various articles/issues.

Time Magazine, various articles/issues.

Newspapers

The Associated Press

The Atlanta Constitution, various editions.

The Atlanta Journal, various editions.

The Baltimore Sun, various editions.

The Chicago Tribune, various editions.

The Nashville Banner, various editions.

The New York Times, various editions.

The Tampa Tribune, various editions.

The Technique (Georgia Institute of Technology student newspaper), various issues.

The Times-Picayune (New Orleans, LA), various editions.

The Washington Times, various editions.

BILL CHASTAIN graduated from Georgia Tech in 1979 with a Bachelor of Science in Industrial Management; his father, his brother, and his two children also graduated from Tech. He covered the Tampa Bay Rays for the *Tampa Tribune* prior to covering the team for MLB.com. Chastain's books include *Payne at Pinehurst, Steel Dynasty, Peachtree Corvette Club, The Streak, September Nights,* and *Hack's 191* (due out in January 2012). He lives in Tampa, Florida.

CPSIA information can be obtained at www.ICGtesting.com
Printed in the USA
BVOW02s2120120913

331048BV00002BA/76/P